IMAGES
of America

HOTEL DU PONT

On the Cover: In 1932, Democratic Party members campaigned to "Stamp Out Prohibition" in an eye-catching, peaceful protest calling for repeal of the 18th Amendment. The demonstration used the main entrance of the Hotel du Pont on Eleventh Street as a backdrop. (Courtesy of Hagley Museum and Library.)

IMAGES
of America

HOTEL DU PONT

Joanna L. Arat

ARCADIA
PUBLISHING

ISBN 978-0-7385-9756-2

Published by Arcadia Publishing
Charleston, South Carolina

Printed in the United States of America

Library of Congress Control Number: 2012937684

For all general information, please contact Arcadia Publishing:
Telephone 843-853-2070
Fax 843-853-0044
E-mail sales@arcadiapublishing.com
For customer service and orders:
Toll-Free 1-888-313-2665

Visit us on the Internet at www.arcadiapublishing.com

Dedicated to the employees, past and present, of the Hotel du Pont. You are the keys to the vibrant history and promising future of the hotel.

Contents

ACKNOWLEDGMENTS

It was a true privilege to write about such a prestigious hotel, an opportunity that would not have been possible without the support of several people. First and foremost, I express my gratitude to my supervisor, marketing and public relations manager Carolyn Grubb, for her encouragement and support throughout this unusual and challenging project. Sharing her continued enthusiasm were DuPont hospitality director, Lisa Bolten; Hotel du Pont operations manager, Annmarie O'Hara-Townsend; my fellow hospitality marketing colleagues, Adam Cofield and Regina Widdoes; and other centennial planning team members.

I am also grateful for the assistance and photographs provided by several key organizations. Special thanks to Lucas Clawson, Judy Stevenson, Jon Williams, and Elizabeth Fite of the Hagley Museum and Library; Ellen Rendle from the Delaware Historical Society; and Kai Lassen, Bob McCoy, and Susan Hastings from the Rotary Club of Wilmington. I also appreciate all the specialty scanning assistance of Dennis Steele and his staff at the Visual Arts Studio, including Jeff Lukowski and Kay Gilligan. Last but not least, special thanks to my editor, Janet Dill, for her passion and dedication in helping me narrate a lasting story.

The content of this book, especially anecdotal information, is based on stories people have told me, notes and brochures, interviews, and historical memorabilia. Unless the image is otherwise identified, the photographs in this book appear courtesy of the Hotel du Pont historic archives.

Introduction

On January 15, 1913, history changed in the city of Wilmington when management threw open the doors of this prestigious, world-class hotel. The city of 80,000 residents had never dreamed of such elegance. This dream-turned-reality, initiated by DuPont executives president Pierre S. du Pont and secretary-treasurer John J. Raskob, evolved from their shared vision: to introduce the grandest hotel, comparable only to palaces and great hotels in Europe, that would serve as a mainstay for world travelers and customers visiting Wilmington to conduct business with DuPont.

Wilmington, at the turn of the 20th century, was growing rapidly, largely because DuPont was expanding from a small company of powder mills and factories along the Brandywine River into a national company that needed corporate offices. The first section of the DuPont Building served as the hub for company business operations. Constructed in 1907 in downtown Wilmington, the headquarters provided offices and meeting space for DuPont executives and employees as well as customers and business colleagues. As the company added to its successes, the need for more office space, overnight accommodations, and entertainment venues grew.

At that time, options for visitors were inadequate or too far away to offer convenience. For Pierre S. du Pont and John J. Raskob, the obvious need opened an opportunity for collaboration in excellence. Decades later, Pete du Pont of another generation said that the hotel was "the greatest gift DuPont could give to this community." It continues to provide a focal point for business, community service, and social events as it moves into its second century.

The visionary leaders chose to construct the new hotel within corporate headquarters, combining business offices, meeting rooms, and fine dining under one roof. Neither budgets nor time restrictions constrained their elegant taste and high standards in both design and construction. They spared no expense during the building of the Hotel du Pont, a building that cost an estimated $1 million. European artists and craftsmen carved, painted, and plastered the 150-room hotel over the course of nearly two years, building up anticipation among local passersby and visiting businessmen.

By the time the hotel opened, guests eagerly awaited the opportunity to savor authentic French cuisine in the elegant Green Room and dance to live music in the distinctive 11th-floor ballroom. On opening day, the building was already considered a masterful achievement of architecture and excellence. Local newspapers estimated 40,000 visitors during its opening. Months later, crowds would gather again for the opening of the hotel's one-of-a-kind theater, the Playhouse, which presented the finest Broadway productions.

Earning a widespread reputation as one of these most elegant hotels of its time, the Hotel du Pont served its initial purposes masterfully. It attracted travelers from all over the world who marveled at its beauty. The location facilitated DuPont business operations. Only five years later, DuPont approved plans to expand the hotel, almost doubling its initial size with the addition of 118 more guest rooms; a new, ground-floor ballroom suite to house the magnificent Gold Ballroom and du Barry Room; and a newly designed, relocated hotel lobby.

In the decades that followed, the Hotel du Pont persevered through dramatic world events including war and the Great Depression. Although neighboring hotels, the Hotel Darling and Hotel Rodney, were not able to withstand these crises, the Hotel du Pont overcame all challenges with outstanding customer service and adherence to world-class standards.

The collection of priceless original artwork, started in the 1930s, provides one example. By internationally renowned artists, the paintings adorning the walls of the public spaces and guest rooms turned a hotel visit into a trip to an intimate museum. Among the most acclaimed pieces are those by N.C. and Andrew Wyeth, who represent one of the most greatly admired and highly regarded artistic dynasties in the United States. Another famous group showcasing paintings at the Hotel du Pont is the Brandywine School of Painters led by Howard Pyle. The works of the Wyeths and Pyle, along with other artists who were born, raised, or studied in Wilmington, contribute to the distinguished Hotel du Pont art collection, one of the most impressive artistic treasuries in the Brandywine Valley, a reputation it still upholds today.

In the 1950s and 1960s, the hotel invested time and money to improve its food and beverage operations, upgrade its guest rooms, and offer additional services that would distinguish it from competitors. Kitchen renovations and expansions focused on refining food service and sophistication. Specialty themed dinners and pre-theater buffets welcomed local patrons as well as visitors from neighboring cities. For casual meals, a new cafeteria on the lower level offered DuPont employees as well as city residents and visitors an alternative to the more formal dining rooms.

Modernizations to guest rooms included television sets, radios, and updated private bathrooms. Other amenities offered employees and guests a bank, brokerage office, airline-ticketing center, pharmacy, newspaper stand, men's clothing store, barbershop, and salon. Exterior renovations added a new, wider marquee that protected guests as they were transported to and from their destinations.

Customer service continued to thrive in the 1970s, when one metric determined that the 20 to 1 ratio of employees to guest, from the bellman who greeted anyone arriving at the front door, to the housekeeper who turned down each bed, to the chef who prepared individual meals, ensured excellence. Ballrooms were booked months in advance. That led management to encourage more and more businesses to host their functions on weeknights.

The hotel celebrated its 75th anniversary in the 1980s with an international flair, hosting a variety of guest chefs and international weeks, featuring countries like Sweden, Japan, and France. Renovations of guest rooms and the creation of the corporate conference center brought the hotel more honors for award-winning room designs in the early 1990s.

Throughout its history, the 217-room Hotel du Pont has welcomed many notable guests, including Nobel Peace Prize recipient Archbishop Desmond Tutu; future and past US presidents, including John F. Kennedy; sports legends, such as Joe DiMaggio; members of royalty, such as Prince Rainier of Monaco; and other iconic celebrities, including Charles Lindbergh, Amelia Earhart, Katharine Hepburn, and Eleanor Roosevelt. Current political and entertainment figures who have attended events at the hotel include Barack Obama, when he was presidential nominee, Vice Pres. Joe Biden, Bruce Willis, Reese Witherspoon, Denzel Washington, and even entire sports teams, including the Tampa Bay Rays and the Arizona Cardinals.

The Hotel du Pont is a member of Preferred Hotels® & Resorts Worldwide, the Historic Hotels of America, and a recipient of the AAA 4-Diamond rating for 36 years, earning it the prestigious honor as the Delaware establishment with the longest tenure on the Four Diamond list. The 12-story hotel remains a proud centerpiece in Wilmington, where it maintains its reputation as the most popular destination for weddings, social functions, business meetings, fine dining, daily afternoon teas, and overnight accommodations.

One

Mainstay on Market Street

Wilmington Trolley. A trolley transported Wilmington residents near the northwest corner of Tenth and Market Streets in 1900. Seven years later, the first section of the DuPont Building occupied this space. Today, a similar trolley conveys passengers to stops throughout downtown Wilmington. The Delaware Transit Corporation reintroduced the trolley in 2002 to evoke the appearance of turn-of-the-century Wilmington. (Courtesy of Hagley Museum and Library.)

Original DuPont Building. Section one of the original DuPont Building stood in the center of Wilmington in 1907. Originally only 105,000 square feet, the building expanded tremendously over the next 25 years. By 1931, the six sections of the structure totaled 643,922 square feet. Today, the building remains the anchor on Market Street in downtown Wilmington. In addition to the hotel, it houses the beautiful, Victorian-style DuPont Theatre as well as a bank, gift shop, coffee shop, and hair salon.

Future Hotel Land. This 1908 photograph shows the Eleventh Street properties scheduled for demolition to pave the way for section three of the DuPont Building, the Hotel du Pont. Construction of the hotel began in 1911, with opening ceremonies on January 15, 1913.

ROOF ANTENNAS. Roof antennas, providing a clear identification of the DuPont Building in the early decades of the 20th century, appear in numerous photographs of the Hotel du Pont exterior. Antennas were clearly visible during construction of the second section. Hagley Museum and Library curator Jon Williams reports that they were added in 1909 in conjunction with the building's very own wireless station that helped transmit messages to ships in the Delaware River. However, it is unclear when they were officially removed because antennas were often airbrushed from photographs. The March 23, 1909, image below shows the wireless station at the DuPont Building. The men in the photograph, however, are unidentified. (Both, courtesy of Hagley Museum and Library.)

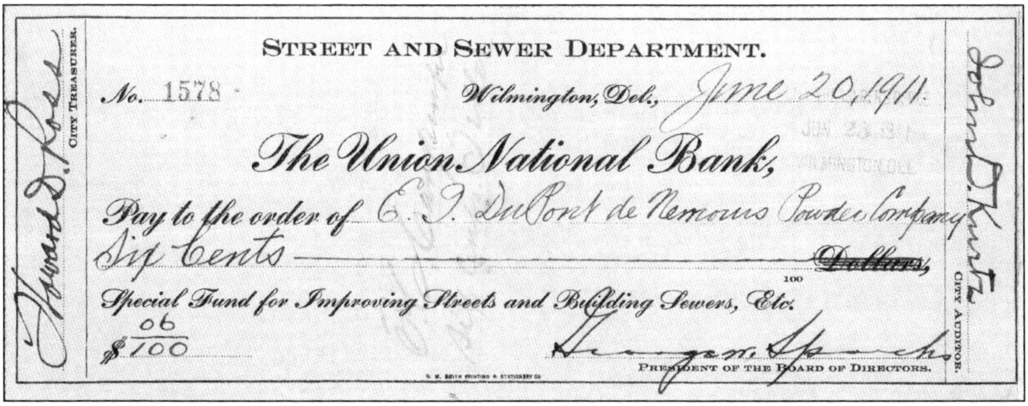

STREET AND SEWER DEPARTMENT.

No. 1578 Wilmington, Del., June 20, 1911.

The Union National Bank,

Pay to the order of E. I. DuPont de Nemours Powder Company

Six Cents ——— Dollars

Special Fund for Improving Streets and Building Sewers, Etc.

$06/100

PRESIDENT OF THE BOARD OF DIRECTORS.

CITY TREASURER.

CITY AUDITOR.

PURCHASED LAND CHECK. The City of Wilmington Street and Sewer Department presented this check to DuPont, in the amount of 6¢, on June 20, 1911, to purchase the strip of land along Eleventh Street. The city planned to widen the street to accommodate the anticipated growth in street traffic following construction of the first-class, modern Hotel du Pont, which maintained the safety values of the DuPont Company.

FIREPROOF STRUCTURE. The third section of the DuPont Building added hotel space to the existing offices. Construction began in 1911, adding 133,500 square feet to the existing structure. The steel framework and concrete construction made it fireproof. The same fireproof materials went into construction of the fifth section, which nearly doubled the size of the hotel by 1919. (Courtesy of Hagley Museum and Library.)

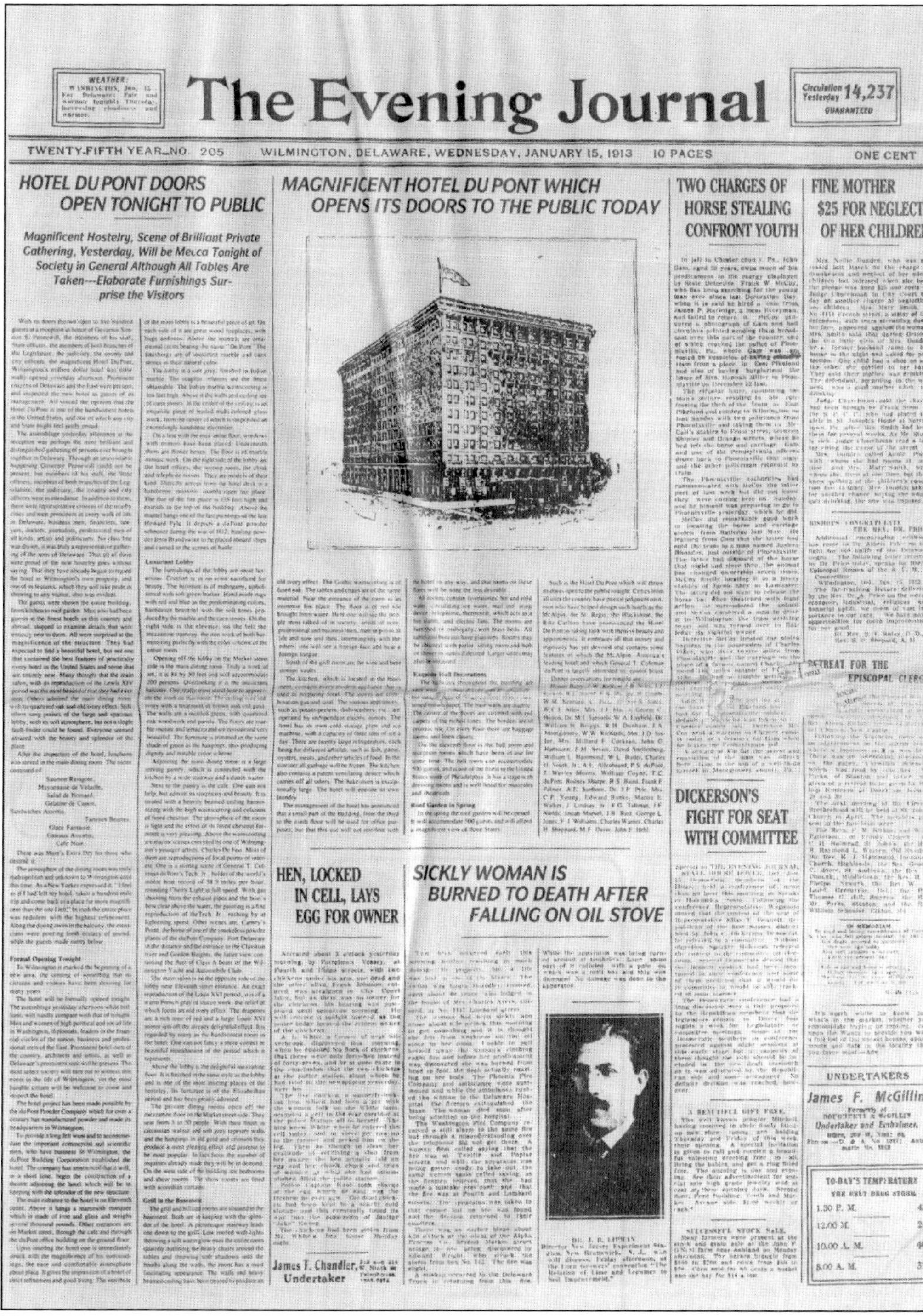

WEATHER

The Evening Journal

Circulation Yesterday 14,237 GUARANTEED

TWENTY-FIFTH YEAR—NO. 205 WILMINGTON, DELAWARE, WEDNESDAY, JANUARY 15, 1913 10 PAGES ONE CENT

HOTEL DU PONT DOORS OPEN TONIGHT TO PUBLIC

Magnificent Hostelry, Scene of Brilliant Private Gathering, Yesterday, Will be Mecca Tonight of Society in General Although All Tables Are Taken---Elaborate Furnishings Surprise the Visitors

MAGNIFICENT HOTEL DU PONT WHICH OPENS ITS DOORS TO THE PUBLIC TODAY

TWO CHARGES OF HORSE STEALING CONFRONT YOUTH

FINE MOTHER $25 FOR NEGLECT OF HER CHILDREN

RETREAT FOR THE EPISCOPAL CLERGY

DICKERSON'S FIGHT FOR SEAT WITH COMMITTEE

HEN, LOCKED IN CELL, LAYS EGG FOR OWNER

SICKLY WOMAN IS BURNED TO DEATH AFTER FALLING ON OIL STOVE

UNDERTAKERS

James F. McGillin, Undertaker and Embalmer

James T. Chandler, Undertaker

TO-DAY'S TEMPERATURE

Time	Temperature
1.30 P. M.	43
12.00 M.	24
10.00 A. M.	40
8.00 A. M.	31

THE *EVENING* JOURNAL. A local newspaper, *The Evening Journal*, continuously covered the Hotel du Pont story, from its design and construction through opening day events and commemorative milestones. This photograph shows the newspaper headline on January 15, 1913, proclaiming the opening day of the "Magnificent Hotel du Pont." (Courtesy of Hagley Museum and Library.)

Opening Day Visitors. According to *The Evening Journal* article that appeared on January 17, 1913, nearly half of the population of Wilmington visited the Hotel du Pont on opening day. The numbers continued to climb in the days that followed, as visitors returned with the hope of catching a glimpse of dinner guests in the Green Room or admiring the Howard Pyle painting that hung in the lobby. News reports described "souvenir hunters"—visitors who walked out with much more than fond memories. Articles in the press stated that hundreds of dollars worth of linens, silverware, glassware, and other ornamental tableware disappeared during the opening week. Thereafter, members of the hotel staff had to keep a more careful watch on the excited patrons bent on collecting extravagant keepsakes of their visits to the hotel. (Courtesy of Hagley Museum and Library.)

Hotel Transportation. Guests who needed transportation in the early decades of the last century could choose from a variety of options. They could wait for the Wilmington downtown trolley (revived for city travel today) or choose a leisurely carriage ride, if they were not in a hurry. This guest decided to ride in a classic Stanley Steamer automobile that is parked in front of the marquee at the main entrance around 1915.

Original Interior Entrance. The original hotel entrance included a revolving door on Eleventh Street. Upon entering, visitors could relax in leather chairs and have a smoke. An ornamental du Pont crest is sculpted into the Caen stone, imported limestone from France, above the fireplace. An Italian mosaic tile floor led to the lobby and into the Green Room restaurant foyer. Below, to this day, local artwork is on display in the lobby. It is also is available for purchase. Patterned-for-safety glass doors replaced the revolving door in the late 1950s to improve traffic flow in the lobby. Today, a small portion of the original mosaic tile floor still remains uncovered in the Green Room foyer. (Below, courtesy of Hagley Museum and Library.)

ORIGINAL LOBBY. Often referred to as "a marble palace," the original 1913 lobby evoked awe and admiration in passersby who were eager to see for themselves the interior of the world-famous hotel. Artistic elements decorated spaces from floor to ceiling, taking the eye from the patterned mosaic tiled floors to the marble front desk, the ornamental chandelier, and wrought iron and brass balustrade of the mezzanine level, then known as Palm Court.

THE ROSE ROOM. The Rose Room, a French salon, was adjacent to the original lobby. This room offered comfortable seating for ladies while their gentlemen partners handled hotel statements. Occasionally, it served as a venue for lectures and dinner parties. The Wilmington Rotary Club and some other organizations held their weekly meetings here. The mezzanine level, or Palm Court, is visible above.

Peacock Alley. Peacock Alley, as it appeared around 1918, included the hotel manager's office. Originally designed as a writing room, it offered guests a place to pen a postcard to a friend, highlighting their stays at the hotel. In the 1940s, management converted this room to a dining room, called the Brandywine Room. It, along with the adjacent Christina Room, evokes the two rivers that flow through Wilmington.

Original Ballroom. Located on the 11th floor of the DuPont Building, the original ballroom was added in the second section of construction, before the hotel opened. This space was used for dancing and entertaining, with six nearby dining areas on the same floor. It is speculated that holding dances for such large groups on the top floor posed a safety hazard. This space, accessible only by elevator, was converted to conference space following completion of the Gold Ballroom in 1918. The image below shows the original ceiling when remodeling teams were preparing a later renovation into the Mt. Cuba and Delaware Suites, which serve as conference meeting spaces today. (Above, courtesy of Hagley Museum and Library.)

Fire Drills. According to guest information cards, the hotel staff tested fire alarms every Wednesday morning at 11:00 a.m. During a 1915 fire drill, testing included the fire hydrants outside the DuPont Building on the Market Street side. If an actual fire occurred, the protection system would sound warning gongs and flash red lights to indicate the location of stairways within the hotel. (Courtesy of Hagley Museum and Library.)

Fifth Section Expansion. Snow covered the streets of Wilmington during construction of the fifth section of the DuPont Building. This image, taken February 1, 1918, shows framework and scaffolding for the Ballroom Suite under construction on Eleventh Street. In addition to the du Barry Room and Gold Ballroom, the fifth section also included 118 new guest rooms and a new lobby. (Courtesy of Hagley Museum and Library.)

New Ballrooms. Above, the Gold Ballroom neared completion in the fall of 1918. Speculation buzzed that the Gold Ballroom was rushed to be ready for an event in November 1918; the rest of the fifth section was completed the following year. The large, arched windows were designed to accommodate a winch and to provide enough space that a car could be driven through them on a ramp. This feature led to numerous automobile shows in the ballroom. The French imported chandeliers had not yet been hung. In the distance, the bronze-railed balconies offer a view of the ballroom from the du Barry Room, shown below, on the second level. Mirrored doors on the balcony separated the spaces, providing capacity for two different functions in the Ballroom Suite to occur at the same time.

Second Lobby Nears Completion. The new lobby is pictured here just before completion in 1919. The materials specified, such as the travertine stone along the walls and floors and the rich Italian walnut for the grand doors, reflected careful selectivity to maintain the elegant but comfortable setting of this public area. The redesign included a revolving door entrance, shown on the right in the middle. The hand-carved plaster ornamental ceiling with colors of antique gold, teal blue, and vermilion crowned the second hotel lobby. A view of the mezzanine level and the new front desk counter is shown below.

SECOND LOBBY COMPLETED. Hotel staff await the pleasure of serving guests in the relocated second lobby. Typical of 1920s hotels, this lobby encompassed two stories, with an ornate mezzanine above the front desk. The new lobby and mezzanine replaced the Rose Room. Today, it remains a centrally located hub between the business offices in the DuPont Building and the Ballroom Suite for social events. (Courtesy of Hagley Museum and Library.)

HOTEL EXTERIOR. The Eleventh Street facade of the Hotel du Pont is pictured here in 1920. Under the decorative marquee on the right was the main entrance into the building, with three Green Room arched windows at the left. At that time, 37 private balconies were available in select suites occupied by permanent residents. The balconies and terra-cotta ornamentation were removed in May 1957.

Winchester Block. This image shows the prominence of the Hotel du Pont from the perspective of Twelfth and King Streets after community and government buildings in the Winchester block were demolished to clear the site for the new post office. From left to right are the Wilmington Library, Delaware Trust, Equitable Trust, Citizens Bank, the DuPont Building, the Hotel du Pont, First and Central Presbyterian Church, and the Wilmington Club. (Courtesy of Hagley Museum and Library.)

Du Pont-Biltmore. From September 1921 until June 1933, the Bowman-Biltmore Hotels Corporation assumed operations of the Hotel du Pont. The property was renamed Du Pont-Biltmore, as it appears on this 1922 envelope. Bowman-Biltmore also operated the Waldorf-Astoria in New York City. When DuPont resumed management in 1933, the name reverted to the original, Hotel du Pont.

THE CITY CLUB. The City Club of Wilmington, incorporated on February 27, 1914, occupied the entire 11th floor of the Hotel du Pont. More than 600 members joined this social club, where they could enjoy spirits on the rooftop garden, a game of billiards or cards, or a men's luncheon among friends. The original ballroom, also located on the 11th floor, offered a convenient venue for large dinners and social gatherings. When the company needed more business meeting space, the club moved out. (Both, courtesy of Hagley Museum and Library.)

Rodney Square Memorial. From its center city vantage point in Wilmington, the Hotel du Pont overlooks the Brandywine Valley, the Wilmington riverfront, and Rodney Square, located across from the Market Street entrance. The statue of patriot Caesar Rodney inspires generations of Delawareans who remember his historic ride from Delaware to Philadelphia to sign the Declaration of Independence. Erected in 1919, the statue stands atop the steps of the square commemorating this patriot of the First State.

NEIGHBORING HOTEL. In October 1936, J. Frank Darling purchased the three-story Elks Club on Market Street and converted it to the seven-story Hotel Darling. He expected the bright neon sign to add prestige to the emerging Wilmington skyline. The Hotel du Pont, just one block south, had a vertical neon sign for the Playhouse. Only eight years later, a New York hotel chain purchased the Hotel Darling, and a new neon sign read Hotel Rodney, as shown below in 1945. Following unsuccessful attempts to sell the property, it was demolished in 1960, and a parking lot replaced it. (Both, courtesy of Delaware Historical Society.)

Permanent Residents. During its first 50 years, the hotel provided permanent residences for many, including DuPont president Pierre S. du Pont. In the mid-1950s, approximately 25 residents remained when management decided to significantly increase rental fees to 80 percent of the daily room rate. For those who had arrived under special fixed rates during the Depression, this increase was substantial. Ralph W. Hayes, the last permanent resident, remained until 1965. (Courtesy of Hagley Museum and Library.)

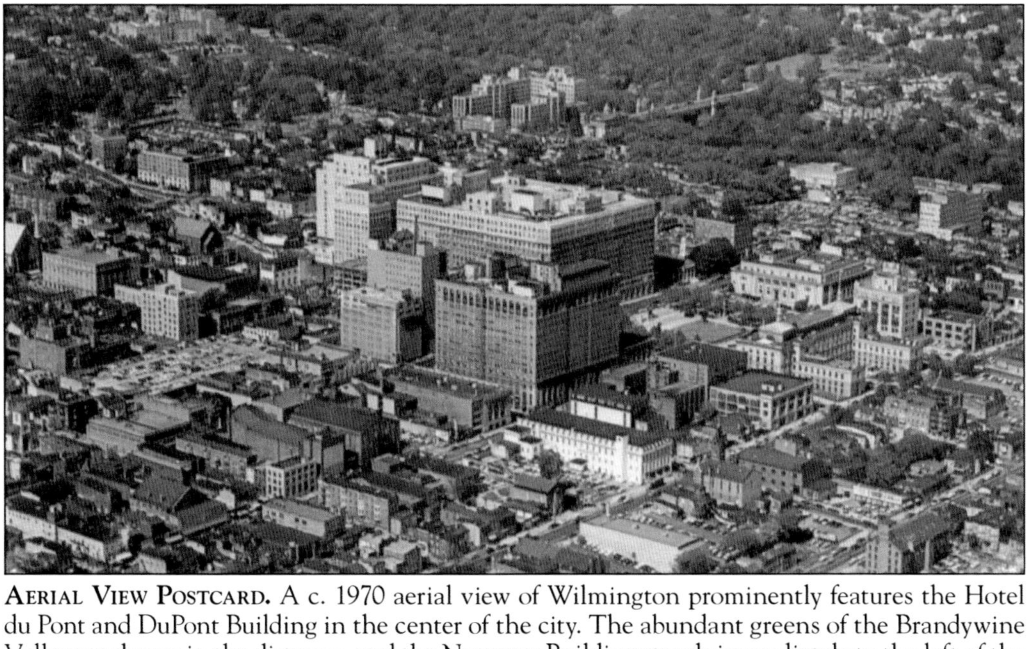

Aerial View Postcard. A c. 1970 aerial view of Wilmington prominently features the Hotel du Pont and DuPont Building in the center of the city. The abundant greens of the Brandywine Valley are shown in the distance, and the Nemours Building stands immediately to the left of the hotel. Rodney Square is located on the right. (Courtesy of Delaware Historical Society.)

Two

At Your Service

Hotel Staff. The hotel reception staff stands on the ballroom stairs for a c. 1920 photograph. From left to right are John Husbands, Joseph Jester, Charles Randolph, William West, Mr. Henderson, Harry Lestardo, Charles Fenton, Casper Fennel, Francis Slavin, and Leon Berger. In addition to welcoming visitors, they had responsibility for assisting with guest check-in and checkout.

KITCHEN OPERATIONS. The dedicated culinary teams at the hotel, including the employees shown above, provide the essential ingredient for flawless operation of multiple kitchens and pantries. Their skills, including food safety and sanitation standards, are the key to outstanding fine-dining experiences. Late-1940s expansions and improvements to kitchen space and equipment, illustrated in the photograph below, increased both speed and quality of food production. One new piece of equipment, a state-of-the-art dishwashing unit, eliminated all traces of the tiniest microbes and bacteria, according to department of sanitation swab tests. Trained dieticians offered insights into healthier food preparation as well, including steaming vegetables to maintain their nutrients.

SEWING KIT. A hotel guest sewing kit from 1928 contains threads in neutral colors, safety pins, a package of needles, and a needle-threading tool. During one prestigious function, a banquet guest requested a needle and thread to sew on a button. A server provided needle and thread, presenting them to the guest on a silver tray with a dome cover.

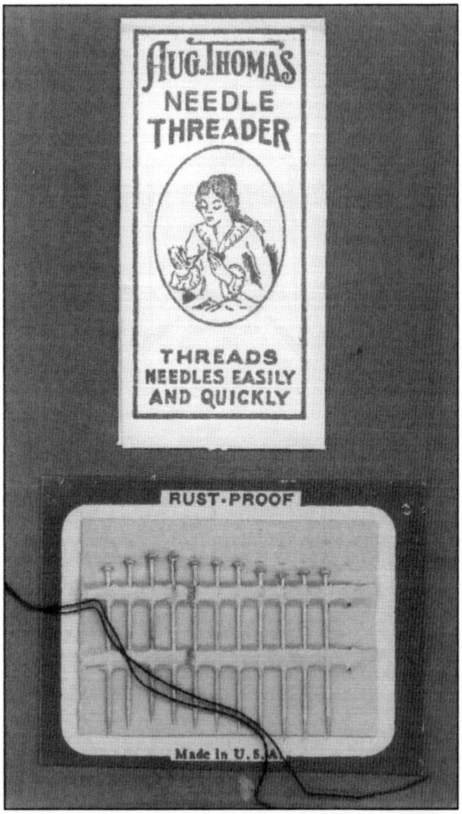

CULINARY STAFF. In the 1940s, culinary team employees break for lunch set up in the kitchen; today, the culinary team eats in the Grill Cafeteria. Documents show that the staff served 405,000 meals in 1946, one of its busiest years, when parties and dinners resumed following World War II.

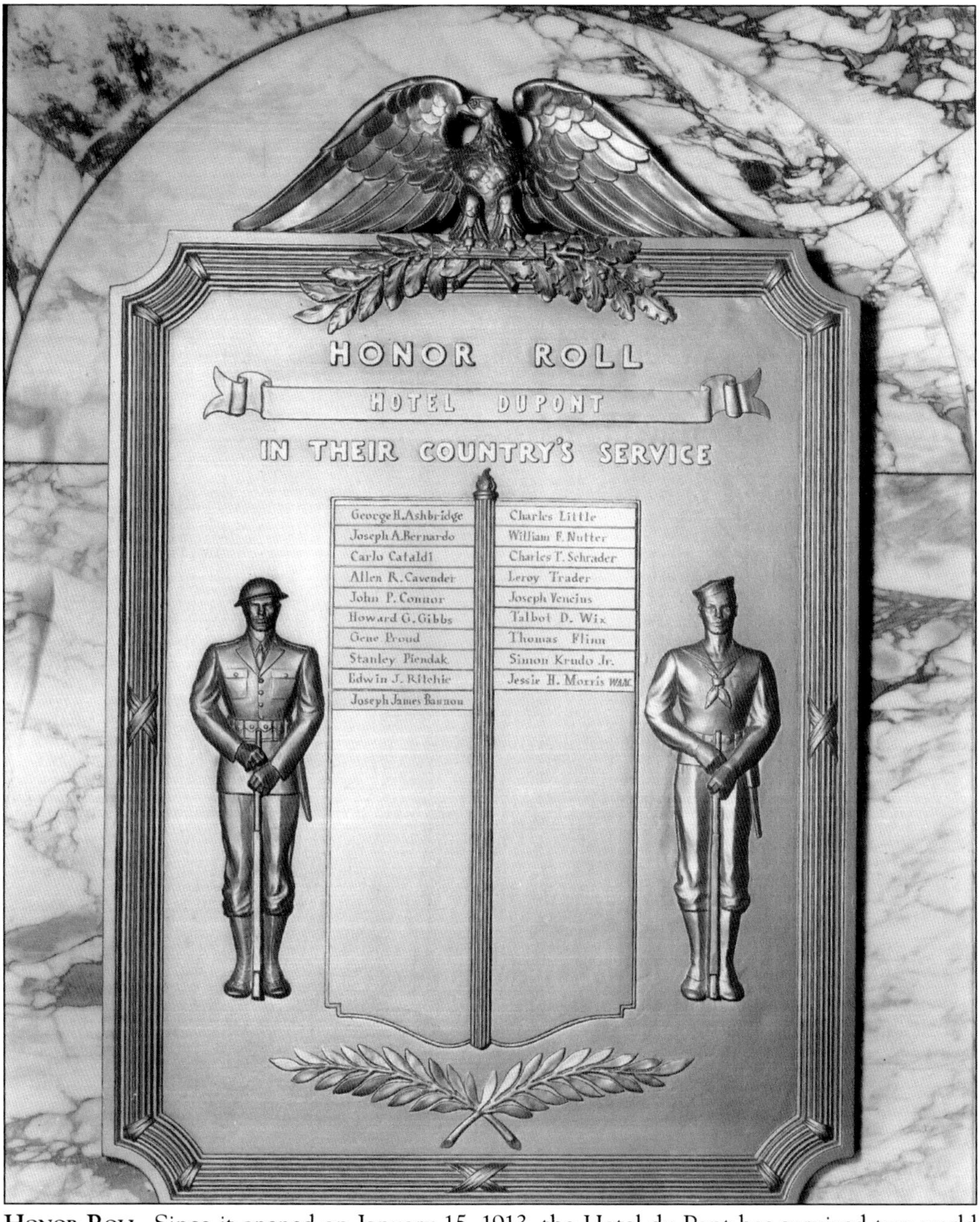

Honor Roll. Since it opened on January 15, 1913, the Hotel du Pont has survived two world wars. However, not all of its employees returned from service to their country. At one time, an honor roll plaque in the hotel reminded employees and guests to be grateful for the service of staff members to the nation. (Courtesy of Hagley Museum and Library.)

Bakeshop Employees. Two bakeshop employees stretch and roll the dough for sweet sticky buns in 1947. Sprinkled with cinnamon and dotted with raisins, these treats are still available in the hotel coffee shop and for the public to purchase from the bakeshop. Bakers today use a dough divider, similar to the one shown in the back right, to evenly cut 36 pieces of dough for rolls. At right, a baker mixes batches of cake batter. Current cooks use a similar whip to mix prodigious amounts of cake batters, meringues, and even to mash potatoes for the Green Room.

Laundry Operations. Above, employees used a new mangle, installed on the 13th-floor laundry facilities on December 15, 1947, to press bed linens. Below, new shirt presses, which went into service the same month, are carefully prepped for ironing guests' freshly laundered shirts. To this day, employees can find the standard operating procedures for all new pieces of equipment in a readily accessible location so they can review the proper procedures at any time. Retraining and audits are performed regularly. Today, most laundering, such as guests' attire, linens, napkins, and sheets, goes to commercial dry cleaners, although the staff washes towels and employee uniforms on-site.

WINE TRAINING CLASS. In 1949, servers participate in training to learn about new wine offerings in the Green Room. A manager reviewed a selection of red and white table wines, including red bordeaux and white burgundies. Today, wine distributors provide educational training to staff, preparing them to create perfect pairings with the meals they serve. The hotel wine inventory, which has received *Wine Spectator* and *Wine Enthusiast* awards for the Green Room, includes some 400 selections, with more than 3,000 bottles in stock.

Employee Safety Meeting. Employees representing numerous hotel departments have gathered in the du Barry Room for a staff safety meeting. They represent the front desk staff, food servers, valet-shop attendants, housekeeping, and bellmen. At DuPont, safety is a core value, requiring every employee from accountants to cooks to attend daily pre-shift meetings as well as monthly and quarterly meetings. A typical safety meeting reviews any incidents that have occurred, reports safety statistics in operations, and rewards and recognizes employees and departments that have achieved milestones in safe days on the job.

Safety Recognition. A large hotel engages many daytime and overnight employees to perform the round-the-clock tasks that maintain high standards of operation. DuPont requires its employees to work efficiently but, more important, to work safely. As a reward for safe practices and zero injuries, employees selected one from a variety of safety prizes, such as those shown in this 1958 photograph. Prizes ranged from household appliances like irons and toasters to leisure products such as barbecue grill tools or a badminton set. Below, management present staff members with their selected prizes for maintaining safe work practices and meeting established safety goals.

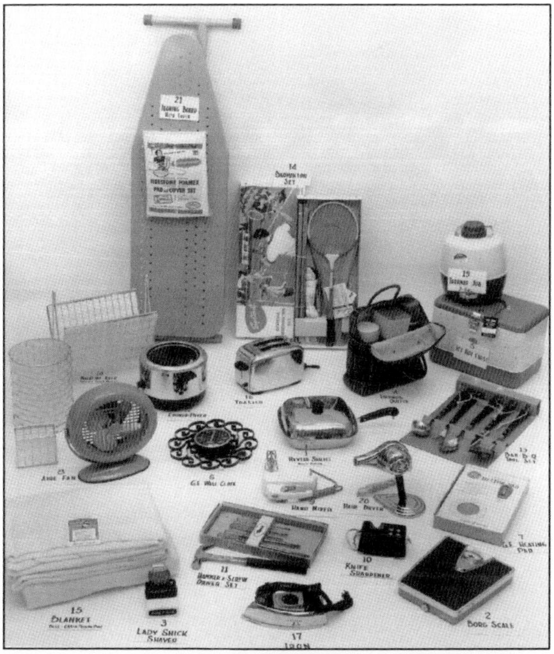

Themed Gourmet Dining. In 1961, the Green Room introduced a series of special gourmet dining events. Servers who were dressed in period costumes delighted guests while remaining in character. The dining series began on January 21, with Colonial characters serving "Old Delaware Dishes" to amused patrons at a dinner titled Delawareana. Below, servers dressed in German costumes toast patrons with mugs of stout for the Bierstube dinner on February 18, 1961.

BANQUET SETUP. Banquet staff pose next to set dinner tables in the Gold Ballroom in 1960. The captain, standing in the doorway, supervised the event, while the banquet servers had responsibility for table setup, food and beverage service, and table breakdown. However, they often went beyond the call of duty to ensure a seamless event. In one case, a captain helped repair a piano in the middle of a concert.

HOTEL DU PONT STORY. Published in 1981, *Hotel du Pont Story*, by former hotel manager Harry Ayres, is the only current published work that tells the history of the hotel. The story relates his insights on progress from the inception of the hotel in 1911 to 1981, covering daily operations, staff, architecture, and service for those 70 years, which contributed to the ongoing, extraordinary reputation of the world-class hotel.

Hospitality Ambassadors. Formed in 2006, the hospitality ambassador team hosts complimentary, monthly events to raise awareness about DuPont hospitality in the DuPont community. Employees from the Hotel du Pont and its sister properties, DuPont Theatre and DuPont Country Club, have hosted backstage theater tours, golf and tennis clinics, cooking and pastry demonstrations, kitchen tours, and lectures offering landscaping tips. In addition, the hospitality ambassadors participate in community outreach projects. Above, executive sous chef David Lattomus provides a grilling demonstration at the DuPont Country Club. Below, actress and comedienne Andrea Martin, second from the left, poses with staff before attending an intimate tea with her show pianist, Seth Ruditsky, of *Andrea Martin, Final Days! Everything Must Go!* Attendees enjoyed lite-bite treats, tea, and social conversation with Martin and Ruditsky, following her May 16, 2012, matinee performance.

Three

An Affair to Remember

Reunion Dinner

Du Pont Gun Club

Saturday, March 15th, 1913

7.30 P. M.

HOTEL DU PONT

Du Pont Gun Club. Just two months after the Hotel du Pont opened its doors, the Du Pont Gun Club hosted an annual banquet for members. The program included popular songs, such as "The Trap Shooters' Song" and "In the Good Old Summer Time." The menu includes oysters, filet of sole, roast turkey, potatoes, and ice cream for dessert.

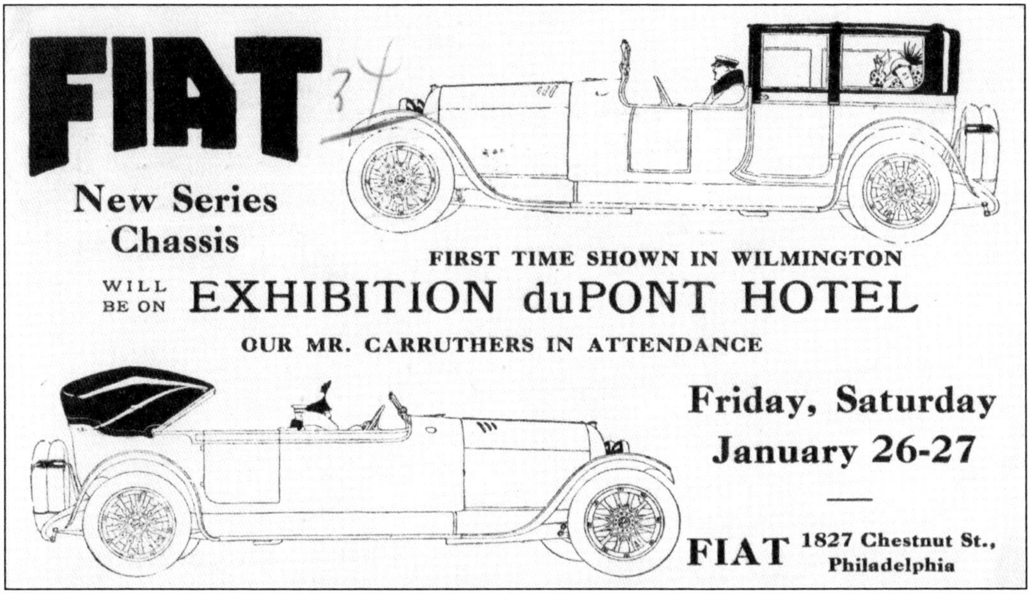

FIAT POSTCARD. Postmarked in Philadelphia on January 24, 1917, this card invites DuPont treasurer John Raskob to the Ford Fiat Exhibition at the Hotel du Pont on January 26. The event introduced the Fiat to Wilmington automobile aficionados. (Courtesy of Hagley Museum and Library.)

MY BOOK OF STUNTS AND FROLICS. This page, preserved in a scrapbook called *My Book of Stunts and Frolics*, includes a 1924 Hotel du Pont postcard. The scrapbook owner lovingly describes the Hotel du Pont as "that darling old structure known as the 'Hotel.'" She gushes over the fraternity dances she attended in the ballroom and the soda shop "where delicious 'cokes' may be bought." (Courtesy of Peggy Mackey.)

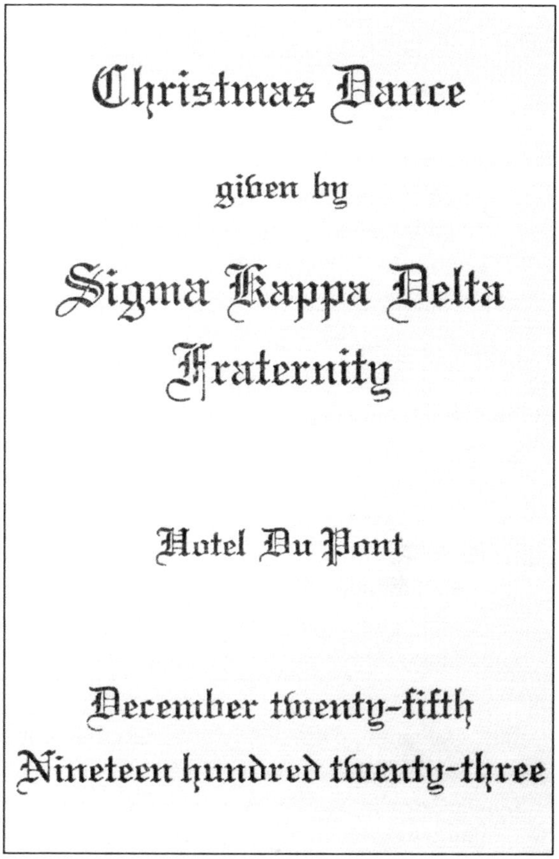

Christmas Dance

given by

Sigma Kappa Delta Fraternity

Hotel Du Pont

December twenty-fifth
Nineteen hundred twenty-three

Sorority Dance Card. This dance card, preserved in a scrapbook titled *My Book of Stunts and Frolics*, commemorates the Sigma Kappa Delta Fraternity Christmas Dance on December 25, 1923. The Hotel du Pont ballrooms hosted numerous balls, many high school proms, community cotillions, sorority and fraternity events, and debutante balls. This card, which came with a miniature pencil attached, includes the names of the gentlemen who requested specific dances with the young lady who held it. (Both, courtesy of Peggy Mackey.)

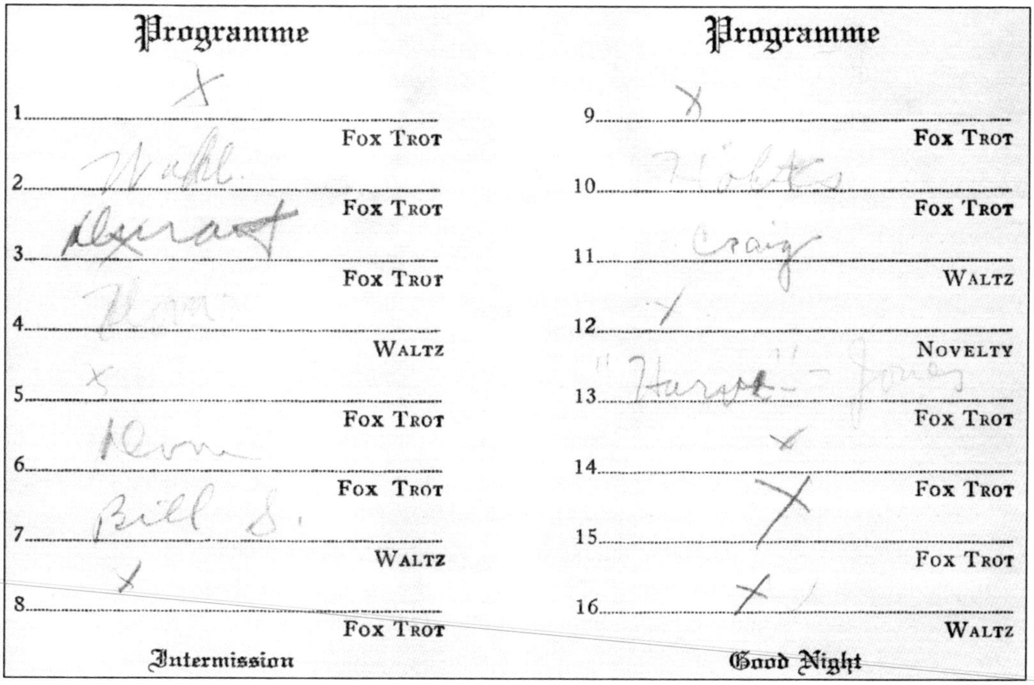

Programme

1. .... Fox Trot
2. .... Fox Trot
3. .... Fox Trot
4. .... Waltz
5. .... Fox Trot
6. .... Fox Trot
7. .... Waltz
8. .... Fox Trot

Intermission

Programme

9. .... Fox Trot
10. .... Fox Trot
11. .... Waltz
12. .... Novelty
13. .... Fox Trot
14. .... Fox Trot
15. .... Fox Trot
16. .... Waltz

Good Night

Debutante Ball. The Gold Ballroom, splendidly decorated for a 1927 debutante party, had fresh floral arrangements and garlands draped over the main chandeliers and sconces on the wall. Other décor for that party includes wooden rails to support elaborate floral centerpieces.

GOLD BALLROOM BANQUETS. In addition to wedding and social functions, the Gold Ballroom has provided a meeting place for many organizations and businesses in Wilmington, among them the Delaware chapter of the American Chemical Society; the Benevolent Pioneers Literary Association, above in 1923; and the First Ladies of Hercules group, around 1930. They all held their weekly and annual meetings, luncheons, and dinner banquets in the Gold Ballroom. (Below, courtesy of the Delaware Historical Society.)

Delaware Flower Show. The Gold Ballroom was transformed into a garden oasis for the Delaware Flower Show on November 16, 1932. Carpet runners and wrought iron gates guided the flow of visitors who enjoyed this floor-to-ceiling exhibit of fresh floral arrangements and garlands. (Courtesy of Delaware Historical Society.)

Masquerade Ball. Photographer Willard S. Stewart provided mementos for costumed guests who attended a Hotel du Pont Masquerade Ball in the Gold Ballroom in 1937. Pictured from left to right are Edmond du Pont, Mrs. Edmond du Pont, Mrs. Henry Silliman, and Henry Silliman. (Courtesy of Hagley Museum and Library.)

Ladies' Reception Room. The Ladies' Reception Room offered a relaxing lounge area for mingling and socializing in the Ballroom Suite. The room is shown furnished as it appeared in the 1930s. A few years later, the staff converted the space for small receptions and dinners, including one for the Pusey and Jones Corporation's basketball team dinner, below, in 1944. Today, this space, just outside the Gold Ballroom, is a popular location for pre-event receptions and post-event desserts.

Green Room Fashion Show. A model poses on a makeshift runway during a 1951 Green Room fashion show. The exhibition platform used here is actually half of a repurposed DuPont Directors' Room table. In 1916, the table was cut in half and reconstructed as two separate tables. The Green Room received one half in 1950.

Carney-Donovan Wedding. DuPont Hospitality employee Mary Donovan Blodgett shared these photographs taken at her parents' wedding reception in the Gold Ballroom on Halloween Day, October 31, 1953. Above, the bridal party, including bride Anne Marie Carney and groom William Joseph Donovan Sr., stands at the bottom of the stairs before entering the Gold Ballroom. Below, guests enjoy a delicious meal while the bridal party stands at the head table on the right with a four-tiered wedding cake prominently displayed. Blodgett describes the joy it brings her to look at these images of her parents, taken in the very building where she has worked for more than 20 years. (Both, courtesy of Mary Donovan Blodgett.)

DuPont's 150th Anniversary. Above, guest speaker Luther Reed welcomes employees and guests at the DuPont 150th Anniversary luncheon for the committee of arrangements. The event took place in the hotel's Gold Ballroom on July 19, 1952. During this anniversary, DuPont established the Hagley Museum. Dedication of the museum in 1957 included exhibits of working powder mills, shown below. (Both, courtesy of Hagley Museum and Library.)

GOLDEN ANNIVERSARY CELEBRATION. A *Wilmington Morning News* article on January 12, 1963, shows Mrs. J.B.D. Edge, a permanent resident, admiring the golden anniversary cake. The Hotel du Pont hosted a dinner dance in the Green Room that recreated the 1913 grand-opening dinner. Two anniversary window displays showcased "then and now" photographs and souvenirs. (Photograph by Frank J. Fahey.)

WEEKEND TOUR PLANS. In 1964, Wilmington newspaper *The Evening Journal* announced new weekend tours sponsored by the hotel. Sales manager Harry F. Green encouraged traveling groups to participate in a Brandywine Valley tour that included weekend accommodations and meals at the Hotel du Pont, paired with visits to tourist attractions in the greater Wilmington area. Privately chartered transportation transferred guests to and from historic sites, including Hagley Museum (pictured above and below), Winterthur Museum, Longwood Gardens, Philadelphia's Independence Hall, and, later, Nemours Mansion and Garden. (Both, courtesy of Hagley Museum and Library.)

GOLD BALLROOM. No first-class hotel would be complete without a lavish ballroom, such as the world-renowned Gold Ballroom, seen here around 1980. From the beginning, the architects and decorators focused on love and women in its design. In fact, it is believed to be the only ballroom in the world so dedicated to love. The Gold Ballroom portrays the skills, expertise, and dedication of artists, sculptors, and woodcarvers from around the world.

THE GRILL SOCIAL FUNCTIONS. Set for an afternoon wedding in this photograph, The Grill has served as far more than a venue for casual cafeteria dining. Planners of weddings, special pre-theater dinners, and bar and bat mitzvahs have envisioned endless possibilities for this room. One banquet manager remembered that The Grill was once transformed into an underground subway station for a New York City–themed bar mitzvah.

Japan Week. To celebrate its 90th anniversary, the world-famous Imperial Hotel in Tokyo sponsored "America Week" and invited the Hotel du Pont culinary staff to participate in July 1981. To reciprocate, the Hotel du Pont hosted "Japan Week" the following September. The culinary team from the Imperial traveled to Wilmington to present Japanese culture through cuisine, fashion, music, and exhibits. The ambassador of the United States to Japan attended the exquisite gala dinner in the Gold Ballroom. Invited guests witnessed the 1,000-year-old, rarely seen Hochoshiki Sword Ceremony. Performing to the music of the 13-string koto, shown above, a trained chef carves carp, using only chopsticks and a sword, unable to touch the fish with his hands. This marked the first time the ceremony was performed outside Japan.

Gold Ballroom Wedding Ceremony. The Gold Ballroom is often magnificently decorated for wedding ceremonies. Brides for generations have made this exquisite ballroom the most popular location in the region for wedding ceremonies and receptions. After the ceremony, the bridal party and guests can be whisked away for a cocktail reception in the du Barry Room, while banquet staff transforms the Gold Ballroom into a welcoming reception site for dinner and dancing.

75TH ANNIVERSARY AUTO SHOW. To celebrate its 75th anniversary, the Hotel du Pont hosted an antique auto show and fair in Rodney Square on October 2, 1987. Community residents, local politicians, and distinguished guests participated in a celebration that featured a stilt-walker, costumed popcorn and balloon vendors, and antique cars. The scene evoked the earlier era when the hotel first opened. The local Wilmington High School band performed at this event. Those attending particularly enjoyed the trays filled with the popular hotel macaroons. Other elements of the 75th anniversary included a period fashion show and a formal gala.

PERIOD FASHION SHOW. As a prelude to the 75th anniversary gala, invited guests selected their gala attire at a period fashion show in the Gold Ballroom held on November 17, 1987. Tables surrounded a long runway down the middle of the ballroom. At right, Lise Monty, editor of *Delaware Today*, wears a c. 1913 period dress to introduce the show, which included men's and women's clothing. The outfits ranged from the Gibson girl look to turn-of-the-century ball gowns. Below, one model struts down the runway in a replica of Audrey Hepburn's costume from *My Fair Lady*. This costume was immediately selected by a DuPont executive wife to wear to the ball.

75TH ANNIVERSARY GALA. The gala ball on January 16, 1987, highlighted the 75th anniversary celebration. More than 300 guests wearing period costumes attended the gala in the Gold Ballroom. The menu replicated the dinner served on opening day, January 15, 1913. After dinner, guests danced to the sounds of Ken Silver and his orchestra until midnight, when champagne and breakfast were served. The group of attendees above poses in period costumes. An entertainer, dressed as a newspaper boy, maintains character as she reads the headlines of the opening day review, as it appeared in *The Evening Journal* in January 1913.

French Week. City of Wilmington mayor Daniel Frawley invited the community to visit the Hotel du Pont for "French Week" from June 26 through July 1, 1989. This week honored the 200th anniversary of Bastille Day, the equivalent to Independence Day in France. In celebration, the staff transformed the hotel lobby into a Parisian café, complete with bistro tables, a fountain, and a model Eiffel Tower. French guest chef André Daguin prepared traditional Parisian cuisine. A polished Parisian hostess welcomed guests with single-stemmed flowers, and an accordion player serenaded each table with French music.

FRENCH WEEK FASHION SHOW. A fashion show of French couture was a compelling event for the "French Week" celebration at the Hotel du Pont. Macy's Northeast provided models who strolled through the French café, dressed in samples from the 1989 fall fashion collections. The show featured cutting-edge designs from Valentino, Claude Montana, and American designer Patrick Kelly.

ROTARY CLUB OF WILMINGTON. The Rotary Club of Wilmington, pictured in 1988, held its first meeting in the Rose Room on December 10, 1914. The group has continued to meet weekly at the Hotel du Pont for the past 98 years. This longevity distinguishes it among more than 34,000 Rotary Clubs worldwide, as the club that has met in the same location longer than any other club in the world. (Courtesy of the Rotary Club of Wilmington.)

Swiss Week. In honor of the 40th anniversary of the Winterthur Museum, above, and the 700th anniversary of the Swiss Confederation, the Hotel du Pont hosted "Swiss Week" from October 21–26, 1991. Events included a Swiss high tea, offered daily. The Winterthur Museum also created a window display for the hotel lobby. One highlight of the week was the Swiss cuisine of guest chef Willi Troehler. Visiting from Mövenpick Restaurant in Winterthur, Switzerland, he prepared international delicacies like Goldenberger wine soup and Kirschtorte for Green Room patrons. Chef Troehler also hosted a cooking demonstration, partnered with hotel executive chef Hubert Winkler. He demonstrated his creamy chocolate soup and presented recipe cards to guests. (Above, courtesy of Winterthur Museum.)

PREFERRED HOTELS® AND RESORTS ANNUAL MEETING. In 1985, Preferred Hotels® and Resorts' general managers and owners worldwide gathered at the Hotel du Pont for a weeklong Annual Managers Meeting. Long a member of the Preferred Hotels® group, the Hotel du Pont hosted the annual meeting for the first time that year. The conference included formal dinners, an off-location picnic, and entertainment from various performers, including the Philadelphia Mummers. For more 40 years, Preferred Hotels and Resorts has offered travelers access to more than 185 of the most luxurious hotels in desirable worldwide locations.

Four

DISTINGUISHED GUESTS

LINDBERGH DAY STATIONERY. The Du Pont-Biltmore Hotel offered complimentary airmail stationery to guests to commemorate Lindbergh Day in October 1927. Pilot Charles Lindbergh had been an overnight guest at the hotel. Covered by nationwide media, the event celebrated Lindbergh's return to Atlanta, Georgia, after making a solo 48-state tour with his plane the *Spirit of St. Louis*.

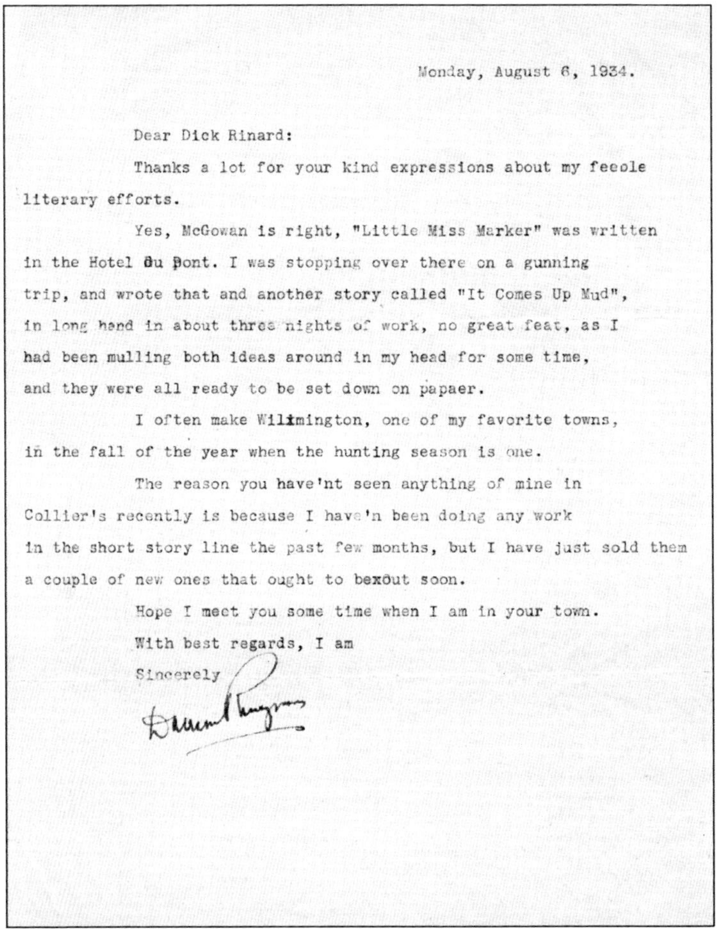

Monday, August 6, 1934.

Dear Dick Rinard:

Thanks a lot for your kind expressions about my feeole literary efforts.

Yes, McGowan is right, "Little Miss Marker" was written in the Hotel du Pont. I was stopping over there on a gunning trip, and wrote that and another story called "It Comes Up Mud", in long hand in about three nights of work, no great feat, as I had been mulling both ideas around in my head for some time, and they were all ready to be set down on papaer.

I often make Wilimington, one of my favorite towns, in the fall of the year when the hunting season is one.

The reason you have'nt seen anything of mine in Collier's recently is because I have'n been doing any work in the short story line the past few months, but I have just sold them a couple of new ones that ought to bexout soon.

Hope I meet you some time when I am in your town.

With best regards, I am

Sincerely

Damon Runyon

AUTHOR DAMON RUNYON. Author and journalist Damon Runyon described Wilmington as one of his favorite cities in this August 6, 1934, letter. He also revealed that he wrote the famous short stories "Little Miss Marker" and "It Comes Up Mud" at the Hotel du Pont during a summer hunting trip to Wilmington. "Little Miss Marker" was later adapted to film. (Courtesy of Delaware Historical Society.)

ISRAEL BOND DINNER. M.J. Ariff photographed guests and distinguished leaders during the Israel Bond Drive Dinner in the Gold Ballroom on June 14, 1955. Honored guest former first lady Eleanor Roosevelt (unidentified in this photograph) attended this dinner that focused on economic growth in Israel. (Courtesy of Delaware Historical Society.)

Presidential Visitors. In 1960, hotel manager John LaMothe welcomes Vice Pres. Richard Nixon and his wife, Pat, as they exit their motorcade. During his visit, Nixon surprised many DuPont employees when he stopped in the Nemours soda shop unannounced. Screaming women greeted him, and the crowd grew so large that his wife could not join him. The Hotel du Pont and the adjoining DuPont Theatre have hosted many other political leaders for lectures, speeches, and overnight accommodations. These guests have included Presidents Taft, Harding, Hoover, Franklin Roosevelt, Truman, Kennedy, Ford, Carter, George H.W. Bush, Clinton, George W. Bush, and Obama.

Mayoral Inaugural Ball. Newly elected mayor John E. Babiarz shares a first dance with his wife, Adele, during his inaugural ball at the Gold Ballroom in 1965. This black-tie affair included honorable guests Gov. Charles L. Terry Jr., future governor Sherman W. Tribbitt, and State Sen. Herman M. Holloway. (Both, courtesy of Delaware Historical Society.)

Swedish Royalty. On April 13, 1988, the Hotel du Pont welcomed Their Royal Majesties King Carl XVI Gustaf and Queen Silvia of Sweden to celebrate the Year of New Sweden. The yearlong series of cultural events commemorated the founding of New Sweden in what is now Delaware. Hotel manager Ferdinand Wieland (left) and Tord Smidt (right) assist a young girl in presenting flowers to the royal family. In the photograph below, Queen Silvia smiles through an array of flashbulbs as she carries her basket of flowers into the hotel. In addition to the royal gala dinner, the royal couple also participated in the nationally televised reenactment of the 1638 landing of Swedish settlers on "the Rocks" at Fort Christina Park.

A Royal Welcome. The Valley Forge Military Academy Band announces the arrival of the Swedish royal couple at the Hotel du Pont Eleventh Street entrance. Pictured below, the royal culinary staff from the Grand Hotel in Stockholm, Sweden, arrived at the Hotel du Pont. On the evening of April 13, 1988, they prepared an elegant meal for more than 500 guests at Their Majesties' royal gala dinner in the Gold Ballroom.

PRINCESS OF THAILAND. In May 1988, Her Royal Highness Princess Chulabhorn of Thailand visited the Hotel du Pont. Hotel manager Ferdinand Wieland assists Danielle Gaessar, daughter of a former hotel employee Chris Gaessar, with the presentation of flowers to Princess Chulabhorn.

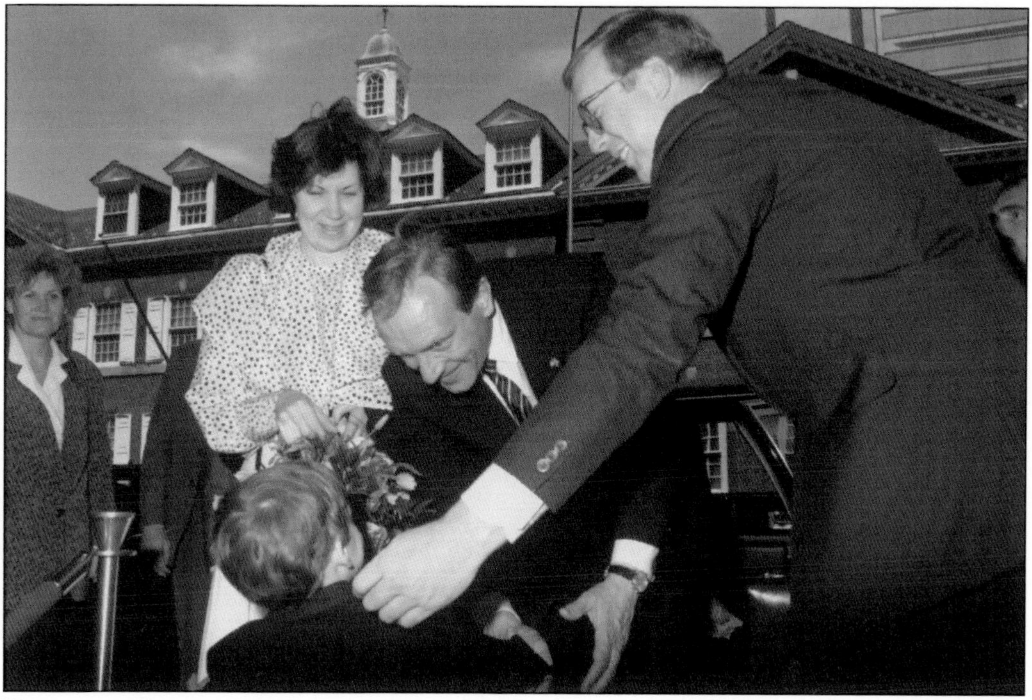

HONORABLE FINNISH GUESTS. On July 8, 1988, Daniel Frawley, mayor of Wilmington (right) helps Rodney Sibert present flowers to the Speaker of the Finnish Parliament, Matti Ahde, and Hilkka Ahde. Whenever possible, management invited the relatives of hotel employees to participate in the role of presenting flowers to distinguished guests. Sibert is the nephew of former employee Maria Kelly.

Rotary Guest Speakers. The Rotary Club of Wilmington has hosted many political leaders to speak to club members about current affairs. Then US senator, now vice president, Joseph Biden addresses Rotary members in April 1989, talking about world events just days after protests began in Tiananmen Square. (Courtesy of the Rotary Club of Wilmington.)

Nobel Peace Prize Recipient. In 2000, Archbishop Desmond Tutu serves as inaugural presenter in the Primo Lecture Series, programs that brought world leaders to Wilmington to focus on peace and reconciliation of peoples worldwide. The series honored the work of the first black Episcopal bishop in Delaware, Quintin E. Primo Jr. Archbishop Tutu received the Nobel Peace Prize in 1984 in recognition of his dedication to freedom and peace in his homeland. (Photograph by B. Proud Photography, courtesy of Cynthia Primo Martin.)

Five

Edible Artistry

Award-Winning French Cuisine. Internationally known for its French-inspired cuisine, the Green Room has earned the AAA Four Diamond rating for the longest consecutive run since 1985. Under the direction of Green Room certified executive chef Keith Miller, certified chef de cuisine David Lattomus prepared this popular surf and turf entrée of butter-poached lobster topping a six-ounce filet, dressed with Parisienne potatoes, frisée, and burgundy demi.

The Green Room. Famous for its exquisite French cuisine and lavish décor, the Green Room remains the only area of the Hotel du Pont that has not been relocated, renamed, or renovated significantly from its original appearance. That distinction makes it one of the most noteworthy features of the hotel. Above, the original 1913 Green Room was surrounded in oak-paneled walls and 2.5-story arched windows that overlook Eleventh and Market Streets. Below, six handcrafted gold chandeliers imported from Spain add to the overall luxurious furnishings. The second-story Musicians' Gallery continues to provide live entertainment for Saturday evenings and Sunday Brunch service. This romantic room once provided a quiet setting when Prince Rainier III of Monaco dined with Grace Kelly, a Hollywood princess, in December 1955. (Above, courtesy of the Delaware Historical Society.)

Green Room Foyer. Entering the Green Room, diners first see the intricate pattern of the original 1913 Italian mosaic tiled floors. These mosaic patterns not only lined the Green Room foyer, but also continued throughout the original hotel lobby, located outside the Green Room. The original hotel entrance was situated where the Green Room Bar is today.

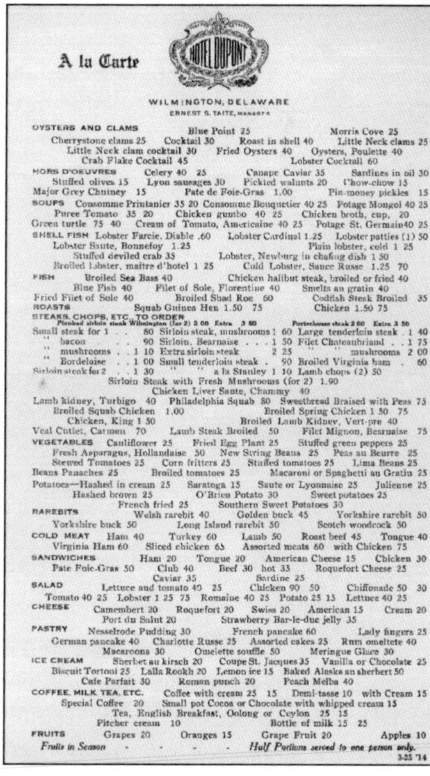

A la Carte

HOTEL DUPONT

WILMINGTON, DELAWARE

ERNEST S. TAITE, MANAGER

OYSTERS AND CLAMS Blue Point 25 Morris Cove 25
Cherrystone clams 25 Cocktail 30 Roast in shell 40 Little Neck clams 25
Little Neck clam cocktail 30 Fried Oysters 40 Oysters, Poulette 40
Crab Flake Cocktail 45 Lobster Cocktail 60

HORS D'OEUVRES Celery 40 25 Canape Caviar 35 Sardines in oil 30
Stuffed olives 15 Lyon sausages 30 Pickled walnuts 20 Chow-chow 15
Major Grey Chutney 15 Pate de Foie-Gras 1.00 Pin-money pickles 15

SOUPS Consomme Printanier 35 20 Consomme Bouquetier 40 25 Potage Mongol 40 25
Puree Tomato 35 20 Chicken gumbo 40 25 Chicken broth, cup, 20
Green turtle 75 40 Cream of Tomato, Americaine 40 25 Potage St. Germain40 25

SHELL FISH Lobster Farcie, Diable .60 Lobster Cardinal 1.25 Lobster patties (1) 50
Lobster Saute, Bonnefoy 1.25 Plain lobster, cold 1 25
Stuffed deviled crab 35 Lobster, Newburg in chafing dish 1 50
Broiled lobster, maitre d'hotel 1 25 Cold Lobster, Sauce Russe 1.25 70

FISH Broiled Sea Bass 40 Chicken halibut steak, broiled or fried 40
Blue Fish 40 Filet of Sole, Florentine 40 Smelts au gratin 40
Fried Filet of Sole 40 Broiled Shad Roe 60 Codfish Steak Broiled 35

ROASTS Squab Guinea Hen 1.50 75 Chicken 1.50 75

STEAKS, CHOPS, ETC., TO ORDER
Planked sirloin steak Wilmington (for 2) 2 00 Extra 3 50 Porterhouse steak 2 00 Extra 3 50
Small steak for 1 . . 80 Sirloin steak, mushrooms 1 60 Large tenderloin steak . 1 40
" bacon . . . 90 Sirloin, Bearnaise . . . 1 50 Filet Chateaubriand . . 1 75
" mushrooms . . 1 10 Extra sirloin steak 2 25 " " mushrooms 2 00
" Bordelaise . . 1 00 Small tenderloin steak . 90 Broiled Virginia ham . 60
Sirloin steak for 2 . . 1 30 " " a la Stanley 1 10 Lamb chops (2) 50
Sirloin Steak with Fresh Mushrooms (for 2) 1.90
Chicken Liver Saute, Chammy 40
Lamb kidney, Turbigo 40 Philadelphia Squab 80 Sweetbread Braised with Peas 75
Broiled Squab Chicken 1.00 Broiled Spring Chicken 1 50 75
Chicken, King 1 50 Broiled Lamb Kidney, Vert-pre 40
Veal Cutlet, Carmen 70 Lamb Steak Broiled 50 Filet Mignon, Bearnaise 75

VEGETABLES Cauliflower 25 Fried Egg Plant 25 Stuffed green peppers 25
Fresh Asparagus, Hollandaise 50 New String Beans 25 Peas au Beurre 25
Stewed Tomatoes 25 Corn fritters 25 Stuffed tomatoes 25 Lima Beans 25
Beans Panaches 25 Broiled tomatoes 25 Macaroni or Spaghetti au Gratin 25
Potatoes—Hashed in cream 25 Saratoga 15 Saute or Lyonnaise 25 Julienne 25
Hashed brown 25 O'Brien Potato 30 Sweet potatoes 25
French fried 25 Southern Sweet Potatoes 30

RAREBITS Welsh rarebit 40 Golden buck 45 Yorkshire rarebit 50
Yorkshire buck 50 Long Island rarebit 50 Scotch woodcock 50

COLD MEAT Ham 40 Turkey 60 Lamb 50 Roast beef 45 Tongue 40
Virginia Ham 60 Sliced chicken 65 Assorted meats 60 with Chicken 75

SANDWICHES Ham 20 Tongue 20 American Cheese 15 Chicken 30
Pate Foie-Gras 50 Club 40 Beef 30 hot 35 Roquefort Cheese 25
Caviar 35 Sardine 25

SALAD Lettuce and tomato 40 25 Chicken 90 50 Chiffonade 50 30
Tomato 40 25 Lobster 1 25 75 Romaine 40 25 Potato 25 15 Lettuce 40 25

CHEESE Camembert 20 Roquefort 20 Swiss 20 American 15 Cream 20
Port du Salut 20 Strawberry Bar-le-duc jelly 35

PASTRY Nesselrode Pudding 30 French pancake 60 Lady fingers 25
German pancake 40 Charlotte Russe 25 Assorted cakes 25 Rum omeltete 40
Macaroons 30 Omelette souffle 50 Meringue Glace 30

ICE CREAM Sherbet au kirsch 20 Coupe St. Jacques 35 Vanilla or Chocolate 25
Biscuit Tortoni 25 Lalla Rookh 20 Lemon ice 15 Baked Alaska au sherbert 50
Cafe Parfait 30 Roman punch 20 Peach Melba 40

COFFEE, MILK, TEA, ETC. Coffee with cream 25 15 Demi-tasse 10 with Cream 15
Special Coffee 20 Small pot Cocoa or Chocolate with whipped cream 15
Tea, English Breakfast, Oolong or Ceylon 25 15
Pitcher cream 10 Bottle of milk 15 25

FRUITS Grapes 20 Oranges 15 Grape Fruit 20 Apples 10

Fruits in Season - - - - Half Portions served to one person only.

3-25 '14

Green Room Menu. An original Green Room à la carte menu from 1914 features a wide variety of offerings including oyster and clam cocktails, simple hors d'oeuvres of celery and sardines, land and sea entrees such as lobster and sirloin steaks, vegetables and fresh cheeses, and desserts. Prices shown range from 15¢ to $2.25.

The Grille Room. The Grille Room, pictured in 1913, offered an informal, cozy setting for food and live music. Red tile floors, a large, wood-burning fireplace, and low ceilings with soft lighting contributed to the club atmosphere. Distinguishing characteristics in the Grille Room include the gnome carvings at the top of the columns. Below, Grille Room servers pose for a group photograph in 1942. A few years later, in the early 1950s, the à la carte service was discontinued. (Above, courtesy of Hagley Museum and Library.)

The Gnomes. This original drawing depicts gnomes enjoying beverages and general merriment as they watch over Grille Room patrons. Artist Raymond Hood designed the gnomes that were carved into the columns of the original Grille Room. The designers of the new room commissioned to have them colorfully painted in 1951. Today, the gnomes are still present in The Grill, located above the salad bar.

Rotary Club Cake. Hotel du Pont pastry chefs stand with an anniversary cake baked around 1940 for the Rotary Club of Wilmington. They sculpted an edible replica of the bell that opens and closes every Rotary meeting.

Soda Shops. At one time, the culinary staff at the Hotel du Pont operated two soda shops, one in the hotel, above in 1920, and the other in the Nemours Building, across Orange Street. In 1946, the two soda shops served more than a million meals to hotel guests, employees, and theatergoers. Neither facility offered table service. Customers ordered their meals and sat at the counter or at one of the tables. The Hotel du Pont pastry shop supplied all the baked goods, including coffee cakes, sweet rolls, pies, and cakes, while the hotel kitchens provided the food, including sandwiches and salads. Sodas were 5¢ each. Managers decided against individual menus and posted the daily specials on boards instead to increase ordering speed.

Brandywine Room. Formerly known as Peacock Alley and used as a writing room, the Brandywine Room opened in 1940 as a lounge-style dining room. It became the Brandywine Room at the same time the adjoining suite, formerly the Club Room, was renamed the Christina Room. These names represented a fast-flowing river that powered the original DuPont powder mills and a slower river that served the early New Sweden settlement.

Brandywine Room Bar. The Brandywine Room also became a popular setting for evening cocktails. A single piece of mahogany formed the 26-foot bar. After one renovation, the hotel donated the bar to former Wilmington mayor Tom Maloney, who enjoyed entertaining actors and guests at his house after DuPont Theatre productions. (Courtesy of Wilmington Public Library.)

THE COPELANDS. Wilmington philanthropists Gerret and Tatiana Copeland contribute to the Hotel du Pont's rich heritage in the arts and fine dining. Their creative Bouchaine Vineyards wines complement elegant dining in the Green Room. Mr. Copeland savors memories of his lifelong visits to the Green Room and shares that it provided an ideal setting for courting his wife. Son of former DuPont chairman Lammot du Pont Copeland, he added "there's no place like home. Wilmington really is the best-kept secret, and my roots are here." (Courtesy of Bouchaine Vineyards.)

SOUVENIR GREEN ROOM MENU. In the 1950s, the Green Room produced four souvenir menu covers. The front cover displays a reproduction of bird prints by F.J. Jacques; the western grebe is shown here. Other reproductions included a bufflehead duck, the king rail, and the ruddy duck. The back of the menu illustrates the Brandywine Valley with a map featuring the landmarks that surrounded the hotel, leaving space at the bottom for a letter about the visit. These collectors' menus reflect the focus on the original art in the hotel collection of paintings and prints. (Courtesy of Hagley Museum and Library.)

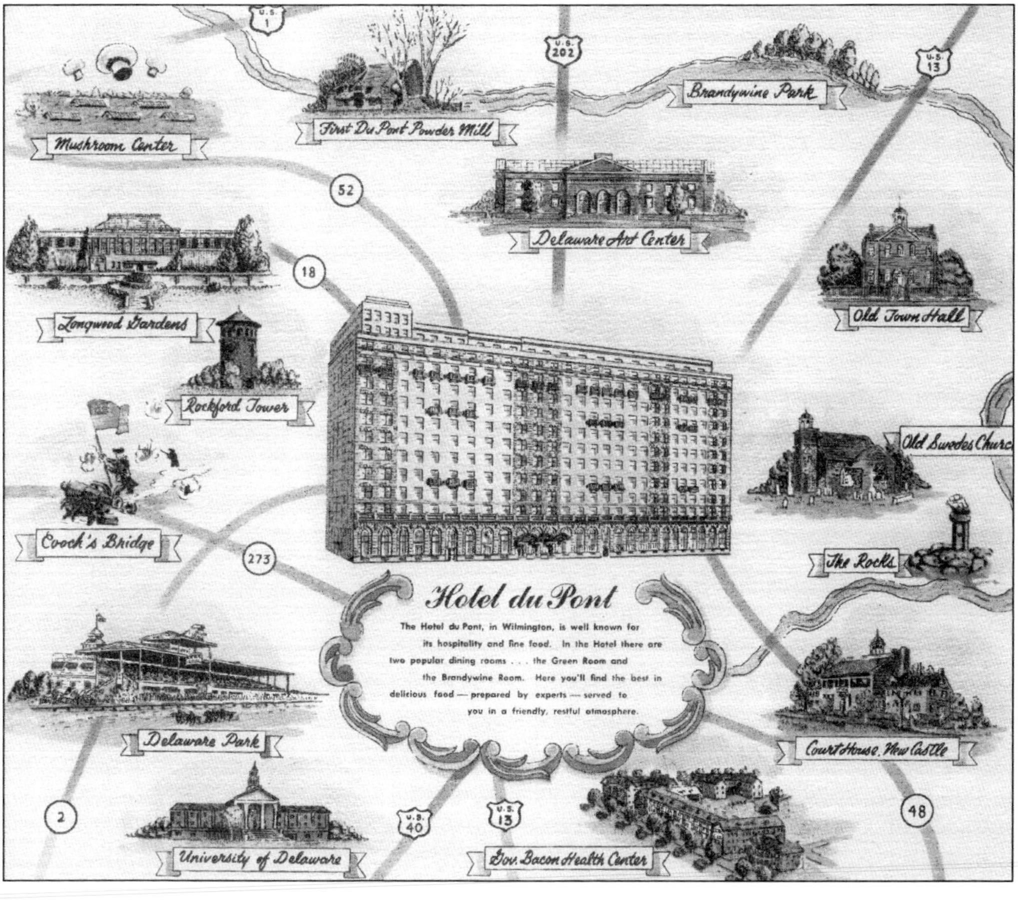

The Grill. Hotel employees enjoy lunch in the renovated Grill Cafeteria around 1950. The Design Section of the DuPont Office Buildings group transformed the Grille Room restaurant into a public cafeteria and renamed it The Grill in November 1951. With seating for 220, it could serve more than 900 people during the daily lunch rush. On opening day, approximately 3,000 patrons came.

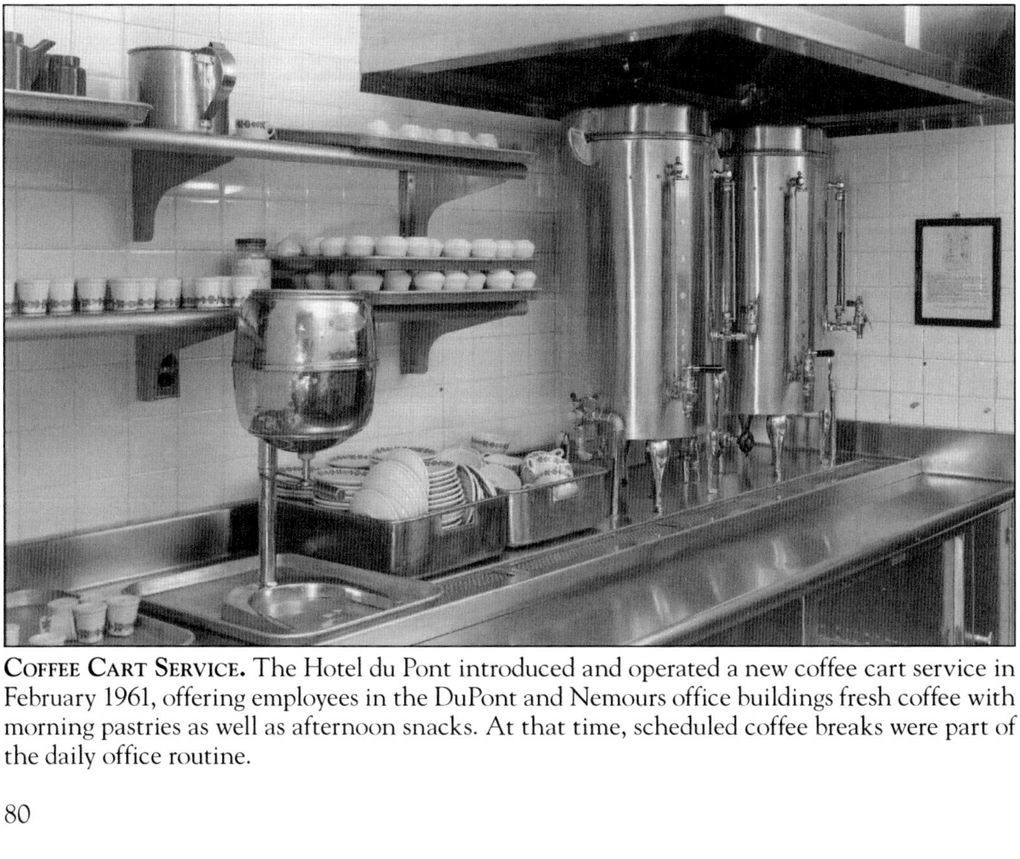

Coffee Cart Service. The Hotel du Pont introduced and operated a new coffee cart service in February 1961, offering employees in the DuPont and Nemours office buildings fresh coffee with morning pastries as well as afternoon snacks. At that time, scheduled coffee breaks were part of the daily office routine.

Green Room Buffets. Executive chef Hubert Winkler served buffet patrons with a smile. During the mid-1960s, the Green Room offered three savory buffets—a Wednesday lunch, a Thursday dinner, and a specialty seafood entrée every Friday evening. These popular events required reservations several weeks in advance. Below, Green Room chefs James Centini (right) and Jim Irby (left) prepared for guests' arrival at a Thursday night buffet. The artistic spread includes a carving station of tenderloin and ham, international and domestic cheeses, a variety of hot and cold salads, chilled shrimp cocktail, a tower of desserts, and much more.

NEUSCHWANSTEIN CASTLE. Hotel du Pont executive pastry chef Joseph Burch poses with his sugar replica of the Neuschwanstein Castle in then West Germany. The construction of this confectioner's masterpiece required 260 pounds of sugar. Robert Cook, an employee in DuPont Engineering, designed the structure that decorated the hotel lobby during the holiday season in 1981.

Hotel du Pont Macaroons. Bakeshop employee Lennie Bungy passed trays of the famous Hotel du Pont macaroons to those celebrating the 75th anniversary. The hotel perfected the recipe and has served these cookies for more than 40 years. Baked in quantity, each batch requires 45 pounds of almond paste, 36 pounds of sugar, and 224 egg whites to produce 3,339 macaroons. Bakers transfer the mixture to a machine called a hopper, which distributes an even portion of dough onto a manually fed cookie sheet. It required four chefs nearly two hours to hand-pipe this dough. Plain and chocolate-dipped macaroons, below, are served in the Green Room and at business meetings. In addition, they are available for purchase at the front desk or in the hotel coffee shop.

Wedding Cakes. Wedding cakes included with all DuPont Wedding Collection packages are designed and decorated in the Hotel du Pont kitchens. It takes approximately six hours for a pastry chef to bake, fill, and decorate a wedding cake. Decorations range from intricate hand piping to delicate sugar flowers. Grooms' cakes, like the Yankee Sports Fan cake below, showcase more creative and amusing approaches to cake decorating. Chefs used chocolate molds for the bottles and sugar for the ice cubes. (Left, courtesy of MK Photography; below, courtesy of Michele Mitchell.)

Jeff Gordon Racecar Cake. To celebrate the DuPont 200th anniversary, the Hotel du Pont pastry team created a life-size replica of professional driver Jeff Gordon's DuPont-sponsored racecar. The bakers made 112 sheet cakes and layered them around a wooden frame, creating a confectioner's masterpiece large enough to serve 2,000 people. Honored guest Jeff Gordon was invited to the anniversary celebration in Rodney Square and cut the first piece from the hood, which was decorated with the DuPont 200th anniversary logo. The February 2003 issue of *Sports Illustrated* magazine features a photograph of Gordon with his cake, giving the celebration nationwide coverage. (Both, courtesy of Michele Mitchell.)

Hotel du Pont Holidays. The hotel has always extensively decorated both the interior and exterior for the holiday season. In this photograph, the culinary team festooned the lobby holiday tree with a gingerbread display depicting the 12 Days of Christmas. Figurines added to each gingerbread house highlight the activity of the day described in the lyrics, such as eight maids a-milking. (Courtesy of Michele Mitchell.)

Six

A City within Four Walls

Custom Amenities. A 1960s marketing campaign featured a tagline calling the hotel "the city within four walls." The plethora of benefits at the Hotel du Pont offered extra advantages to guests. They included real estate offices, a theater, airline ticket office, drugstore, smoke shop, stock brokerage offices, flower shop, gentlemen's barbershop, jewelry shop, and Wilmington Trust Bank at the corner of Tenth and Market Streets. (Courtesy of Delaware Historical Society.)

The Playhouse. In 1913, DuPont executives John J. Raskob, Pierre S. du Pont, and R.R.M. Carpenter launched plans to build a theater in Wilmington large enough to accommodate any Broadway show. The theater, shown above nestled in the alley called Pinkett's Court between Tenth and Eleventh Streets, provided the third special benefit for guests, a venue for live entertainment, along with luxurious accommodations and exquisite dining under one roof. Constructed in only 150 days, the Victorian-style Playhouse received praise as one of most comfortable theaters in the country. It is also among the largest and, certainly, the safest. Although the name was changed in 2003 to the DuPont Theatre, it has delivered 100 continuous seasons of Broadway entertainment, earning it accolades as the oldest continuously operating legitimate theater in the nation. (Both, courtesy of Hagley Museum and Library.)

Ladies' Hat Shop. When modifications to the hotel included moving the lobby, architects split the original lobby space into a two-level soda shop and ladies' hat shop. This photograph shows the hat shop as it appeared in 1920, when women wore hats everywhere. It carried the latest and most fashionable designs. Reminders of the original hotel lobby, such as the fireplace with the du Pont crest carved into the mantel, pinpoint the location of the hat shop.

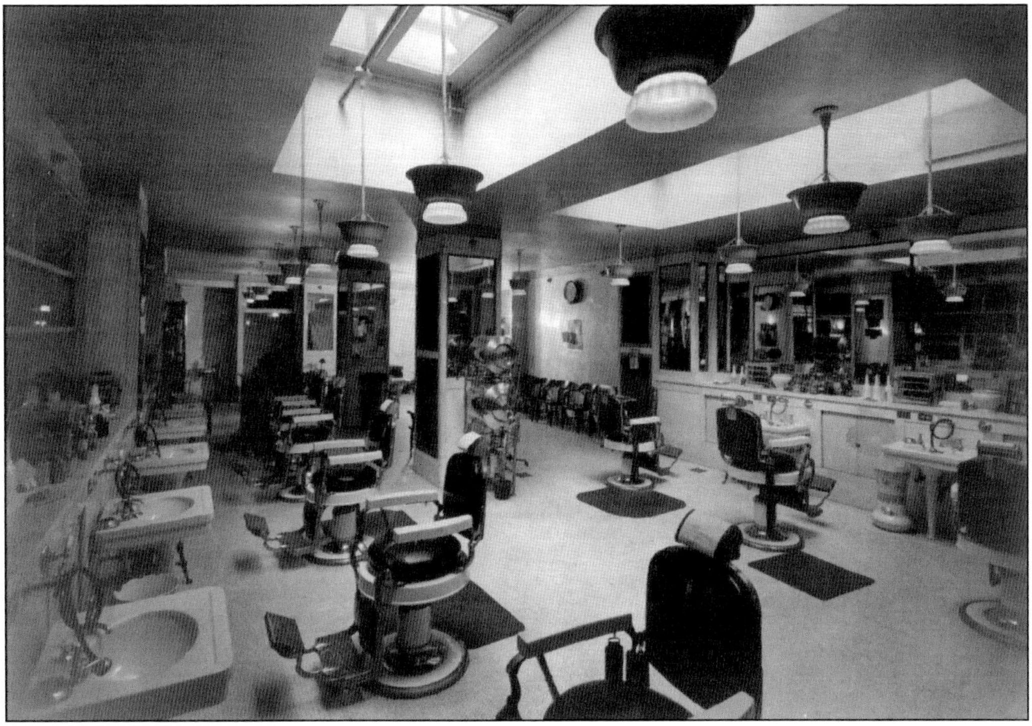

Gentlemen's Amenities. Male visitors and employees could enjoy a haircut and hot shave in the hotel barbershop (above), or they could purchase stylish apparel at the Mansure and Prettyman Men's Store, located on the ground floor. The c. 1920 window display showcases hats, ties, and other men's furnishings for sale. Suits, shirts, and casual clothing were available as well. (Both, courtesy of Hagley Museum and Library.)

The Newsstand. When the newsstand (above) opened its doors for business, the first customers included employees as well as hotel guests. As the store name indicated, this 1940s shop sold newspapers as well as magazines, tobacco products, and small gift items. Before its official opening, a temporary shop (below) was available in the lobby. It offered convenience for guests and employees, but it did not suit the atmosphere nor match the elegance of the setting.

Hotel Gift Shop. In 1935, the hotel gift shop (above) offered decorative items for the home, including vases, statues, books, and serving platters. A Kodak sign advertises the sale of cameras, film, and photography equipment as the popularity of amateur picture taking soared. In the 1960s, a new gift shop, the Beehive, opened on the ground level (below). Some described it simply as a smoke shop, although it carried a variety of other merchandise as well. Today, the Hospitality Gift Shop is fully stocked to accommodate the needs of overnight guests, restaurant patrons, and employees, providing sundries, personal items, stamps, and souvenirs. (Below, courtesy of Hagley Museum and Library.)

J.E. Caldwell and Co. The hotel facilities included a prestigious jewelry shop, J.E. Caldwell and Company, founded in Philadelphia. The shop offered quality jewelry and gifts for hotel guests and community patrons. Lighted display cases lined the walls and stood freely in the store, showcasing luxury items including crystal vases, bowls, china, silver flatware and tea service, candlestick holders, statues, and watches. It remained on the ground floor of the building from 1967 until 2010.

Lobby Lounge Drawing. This c. 1981 drawing depicts the proposed Lobby Lounge in the Hotel du Pont. The lounge offered an intimate setting for cocktails and light meals. A grand piano provided relaxing musical entertainment before dinner or a show at the DuPont Theatre, located down the corridor and to the right.

Lobby Lounge Completed. Visitors and employees often described the newly designed Lobby Lounge, completed in 1983, as the "living room" of the hotel. Formal yet comfortable, its atmosphere set the tone for elegant afternoon high tea or a tranquil spot to relax after a day of sightseeing in the Brandywine Valley.

Seven

The Muse and the Music

Gold Ballroom. Many visitors consider the Gold Ballroom's rare sgraffito-patterned walls, pictured here in 1930, a work of art. Designer Duncan Smith's team of 30 artisans etched patterns into five layers of colored plaster to create breathtaking designs and complex texture on the walls. Equally extraordinary are the 20 carved medallions positioned between each arched window, representing famous women in history such as Helen of Troy and Pocahontas. (Courtesy of the Delaware Historical Society.)

Club Room Batik. An especially designed, silk-dyed batik hung prominently over the Club Room fireplace in 1913. Artist Arthur Crisp titled his masterpiece *A Legend of Hospitality.* The batik received rave reviews for being one of the most ambitious pieces of its kind, because it used dyes of 13 different colors. In 1919, when Mrs. H.P. Whitney's New York studio displayed it, a *New York Times* art critic said, "The paintings fade into inconspicuousness in the company of this gorgeous fabric made for a hotel in Wilmington." The Club Room originally served as a formal cocktail lounge; however, the staff could convert it easily for private dinners and events as shown here.

CLUB ROOM CEILING. Some hotel guests consider the one-of-a-kind Tiffany ceiling in the Club Room as impressive as the artwork on the walls. The three glass skylights depict marine images—a ship of the Lord De La Warr period, a warship from 1812, and a 20th-century destroyer. (Courtesy of Hagley Museum and Library.)

THE ORPHEUS CLUB. The 75 members of the Orpheus Club of Wilmington prepared to sing in the Gold Ballroom around 1930. The all-male singing group commissioned this Ellis Studio photograph at one Hotel du Pont performance. (Courtesy of Delaware Historical Society.)

Art Collection. The Hotel du Pont upheld high standards in developing an art collection, which management started in 1937. While many other luxurious hotels hang reproductions, the Hotel du Pont is one of the rare hotels in the world that showcases local, original works of art in its public and private places, particularly in dining rooms and conference spaces. At one time, paintings also hung in guest rooms and were available for purchase. The hotel has supported the Studio Group's artist gallery since 1964. A showcase in the lobby offers a new original painting by a local artist, which is available for purchase by hotel guests or community visitors. To increase exposure and sales for local artists, the selection changes each week.

THE CHRISTINA ROOM. Paneled in Italian walnut, the Christina Room, formerly the Club Room, has carvings of beavers, pelicans, and wheels, symbolizing hard work. An intimate setting for private functions, the Christina Room today displays priceless paintings of local artists, including three generations of Wyeths—N.C., Andrew, and Jamie.

THE ISLAND FUNERAL. Artist N.C. Wyeth not only illustrated famous children's books, including the Scribner Classic edition of *Treasure Island*, but also painted this masterpiece, *Island Funeral*. A student of Howard Pyle, he expanded from illustrations, extending his interest to interpreting landscapes near his summer home in Maine. This oil and tempura painting depicts friends and family members gathered at Teel Island to pay their respects to his friend Capt. John Teel.

Christmas Shop. In the late 1930s, the hotel began building its collection of original art purchased at local art shows and other exhibitions, like the annual Christmas Shop. Beginning in 1924, the Christmas Shop committee hosted this annual sale in the Gold Ballroom. In 1949, the group initiated a show of watercolors, displayed in the hotel lobby. It was a successful venture for local artists, the committee, and the hotel. (Courtesy of Hagley Museum and Library.)

Big Band Music. Live music by groups like this five-person band brightened spirits weekly at the Hotel du Pont. The Gold Ballroom and du Barry Room have hosted countless social functions since they opened in 1919. Today, many social functions continue in the Gold Ballroom, including the Bachelor's Ball, Holly Ball, cotillions, the Grand Gala, and high school cotillions and proms. Local entertainment companies such as Brandywine Valley Talent offer Hotel du Pont clients a variety of bands to book for social or business functions. One of the most frequently requested groups, the award-winning Philadelphia band Jellyroll, entertained Pres. George W. Bush and his guests at the 2007 Congressional Ball at the White House.

Spanish Week. Honoring the 75th anniversaries of both hotels, the Hotel du Pont hosted the Palace Hotel of Madrid for "Spanish Week," September 26–October 1, 1988. Visiting guest chef Francisco Rubio Sánchez prepared traditional Spanish cuisine for dining patrons. Former Barcelona University band Los Tunos, joined by flamenco dancers, entertained dining patrons, hotel guests, and the Wilmington community in presenting several one-hour shows. They performed in the Hotel du Pont lobby (above), at the A.I. DuPont Children's Hospital, and on Rodney Square, located outside the hotel Market Street entrance (below).

Eight

HOME SUITE HOME

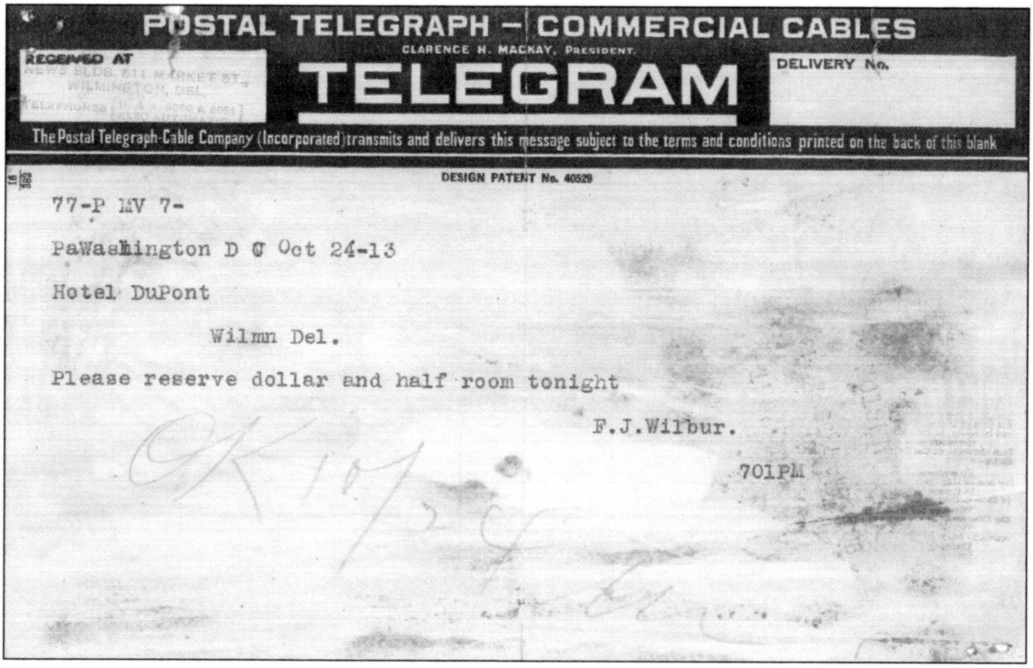

POSTAL TELEGRAPH — COMMERCIAL CABLES

CLARENCE H. MACKAY, PRESIDENT.

RECEIVED AT

TELEGRAM

DELIVERY No.

The Postal Telegraph-Cable Company (Incorporated) transmits and delivers this message subject to the terms and conditions printed on the back of this blank

DESIGN PATENT No. 40529

77-P MV 7-

PaWashington D C Oct 24-13

Hotel DuPont

Wilmn Del.

Please reserve dollar and half room tonight

F.J.Wilbur.

701PM

RESERVATION TELEGRAM. Some 10 months after opening day, F.J. Wilbur from Washington, DC, sent this telegram to the Hotel du Pont, reserving a room for the evening of October 24, 1913. At this time, the hotel only offered 150 guest suites; the room he requested cost $1.50.

THE HOTEL DUPONT
EUROPEAN
ERNEST S. TAITE, MANAGER.

The hotel is not responsible for the loss of articles from rooms. Steel boxes are provided in the office for the safe keeping of valuables.

Guests taking rooms without having baggage will invariably be required to pay for them in advance.

LOCK YOUR DOOR WHEN GOING OUT AND LEAVE KEY AT OFFICE

All bills payable weekly.

Do not leave key on the outside of door.

Guests will be charged for their rooms until notice is given at the Office of their desire to vacate them.

Carriages and Taxi Cabs can be had at all hours upon application to Front Office.

We would advise patrons when expecting callers to notify the office of their whereabouts in the hotel, and thus enable call boys to locate them quickly.

Public Stenographers Office in Writing Room.

YOUR KEY LOCKS THIS DOOR MAIDS KEY WILL NOT OPEN IT

It is earnestly requested that any neglect or incivility on the part of the servants may be promptly reported at the Office.

Hotel duPont Company

AN ACT CONCERNING HOTEL KEEPERS

Chapter 417, Volume 14, Laws of Delaware.

Section 1. Whenever the proprietor or proprietors of any hotel, inn or boarding house, shall provide a good, sufficient and secure safe, in the office of such hotel, or other convenient place, for the safe keeping of any money, goods, jewelry and valuables belonging to the guests and boarders of such hotel, inn or boarding house, and shall notify the guests and boarders thereof by placing in every lodging room, parlor and public hall and other conspicuous places, printed cards or notices stating the fact that such safe is provided in which such goods, jewelry and valuables may be deposited; and that the proprietor or proprietors thereof will not be responsible for said money, goods, jewelry and valuables unless deposited in said safe, and if any such guest or boarder shall neglect to deposit such money, goods, jewelry or valuables in such safe the proprietor or proprietors aforesaid shall not be liable to any loss of such money, goods, jewelry or valuables sustained by such guest by theft or otherwise.

FIRE ALARM

In the event of fire, an alarm will be rung on the gongs located in the corridors. Fire alarm tested every Wednesday at 11 A. M.

RED LIGHTS indicate the location of stairways.

GUEST INFORMATION CARDS. Hotel manager Ernest Taite created a guest information card in 1914 to highlight general hotel guidelines for overnight guests and residents. It describes the availability of taxi cabs and carriages out front, requests that the arrival of any guests be communicated to the front office, recommends securing valuables in the front office safes, and explains the process for properly paying bills each week.

ROOM TARIFF. A 1916 Hotel du Pont brochure highlights benefits, including all rooms equipped with lavatories, hot and cold water, and circulating ice water. Room tariffs ranged from $1.50 per night for a single occupancy room without a bath to $10 per night for a double occupancy suite with a parlor, bedroom, and bath. By 1936, as this statement shows, prices increased to $6 per night.

239 CHRISTIE J W MR & MRS 6 00
9/12/36 11 21 PM

SILVER SPRINGS MD

Wilmington, Del.

No. 91403

MEMO.		DATE	EXPLANATION	CHARGES	CREDITS	BAL. DUE
	1	SEP12-36	ROOM	* 6.00		* 6.00
	2					
	3					
	4					
	5					
	6					
	7		PAID			
	8					
	9		SEP 13 ... 36			
	10					

Directors' Room Table. The walnut paneled Directors' Room (above) on the eighth floor in the fourth section of the DuPont Building was the location of a 24-foot directors' table from 1916 to 1930, shown here. After the completion of the sixth and final section of the building, the Directors' Room moved to the ninth floor. At that time, the table was cut in half and refinished to create two smaller tables. The DuPont Legal Library received half the table, while the other furnished the Executive Committee Room from 1930 to 1949. In 1950, the company presented it to the Green Room. It is shown (below) in 1951. (Both, courtesy of Hagley Museum and Library.)

BALLROOM SUITE ENTRANCE. Twelve-foot, hand-carved Italian walnut doors separate daily business in the hotel lobby from celebrations in the ballrooms. The Ballroom Suite, completed in 1919, contains the du Barry Room and the Gold Ballroom. The cornucopias carved into the stone above the doorways symbolize that visitors are entering a feast. The walnut grandfather clock, left, purchased in 1918, remains in the lobby today. (Courtesy of Hagley Museum and Library.)

BALLROOM SUITE EXIT. This image shows the opposite side of these walnut doors, as viewed from the stair landing. Travertine floors and walls in the lobby meet a gold-coffered ceiling. Intricate metal railings frame Roseal marble staircases that lead up to the du Barry Room or down to the Gold Ballroom. Squirrels carved into the stone above the doorway signify that visitors will be returning to the working world.

Ballroom Suite Lobby. This panoramic view of the Ballroom Suite lobby highlights the marble staircase. Records indicate that one piece of marble provided stone for the stairways that sweep up to the du Barry Room and down to the Gold Ballroom lobby. An exterior entrance on the right, referred to as the social entrance, allows guests to leave the Ballroom Suite without returning to the lobby, a convenience that was not available in the 11th-floor ballroom.

STAIR LANDING. This image depicts the stair landing, an area in the Ballroom Suite added in the fifth section of the DuPont Building. Hotel manager Ernest S. Taite printed this photograph in a 1920s Hotel du Pont brochure. Beyond the walnut doorways is the hotel lobby. The du Barry Room is at the top of the marble stairways.

Du Barry Room. Rumored to be named for Madame du Barry, this ballroom showcases a beautiful crystal chandelier imported from Yugoslavia. Although this chandelier is not original to the room, its addition enhances the overall beauty of the space. Architecturally and aesthetically, the du Barry ballroom reflects the Empire period, providing a perfect setting for a wedding ceremony, intimate reception, dinner, or formal business meeting.

Ballroom Suite Foyer. In 1920, the foyer of the Ballroom Suite provided a comfortable and restful space, perhaps intended to replace the Rose Room. It had floral-patterned upholstery on easy chairs and lampshades, creating a welcoming atmosphere before, during, or after a social function. The drawn drapes cover entrances to the Gold Ballroom.

Moderne Suite. This Moderne Suite at the Du Pont-Biltmore, pictured in 1927, offered an efficient room for double occupancy. Twin beds, dressers, nightstands, vanity table with sterling silver brush and comb, and private baths provided a pleasant retreat. The room tariff was $4.50 per night. Today, the 11 suites in the hotel all include at least one bedroom, 1.5 bathrooms, and separate living and dining areas. Reese Witherspoon, Bob Hope, Elizabeth Taylor, Bruce Willis, and many other famous entertainers have occupied a suite at the Hotel du Pont.

Single Room. This single room at the Du Pont-Biltmore, pictured here in 1928, was known as a Bachelor Room. A color palette of tan, orange, deep red, and black decorated the walls and accessories. The pillows on the daybed were of rayon plush. A secretary's desk with chair and artwork on the walls made this rather small room feel more spacious.

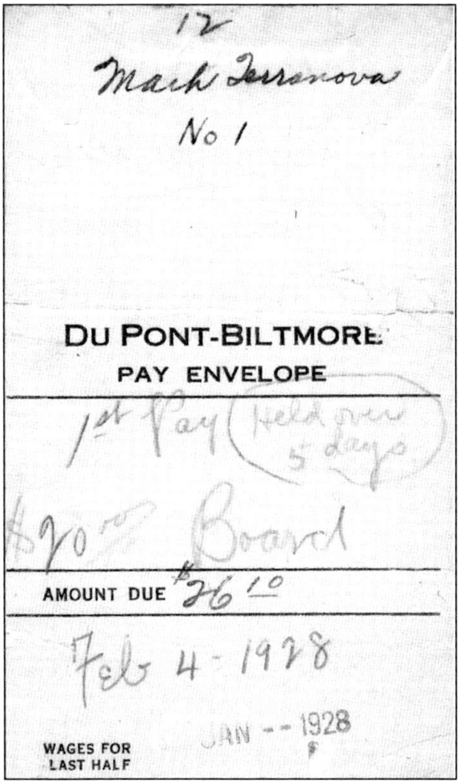

12

No 1

DU PONT-BILTMORE

PAY ENVELOPE

1st Pay (Held over 5 days)

$20.00 Board

AMOUNT DUE $26.10

Feb 4 - 1928

WAGES FOR LAST HALF

JAN -- 1928

Du Pont-Biltmore Pay Envelope. The front and back of a pay envelope from February 4, 1928, spell out a weekly boarding rate of $20. The back of the envelope lists additional items purchased during the week and added to the final statement. They include toothpaste for 35¢, four pairs of stockings for 50¢, and shoes for $3.50.

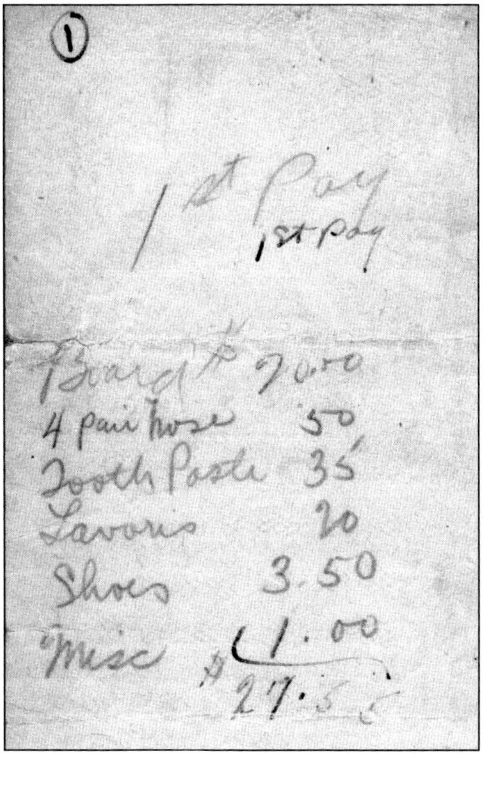

1

1st Pay

1st Pay

Board	$20.00
4 pair hose	50
Tooth Paste	35
Favors	20
Shoes	3.50
Misc	1.00
	$27.55

Front Entrance Postcard. This vertical postcard depicts the front entrance of Hotel du Pont in the 1940s. A longer entrance marquee that is more modern replaced this original, ornate design in 1958. The reverse side of the postcard describes the Hotel du Pont as the "Business, Civic, and Social Center of Wilmington." (Courtesy of Delaware Historical Society.)

GOLD BALLROOM RENOVATIONS. Management commissioned renovations to the Gold Ballroom in 1946 in anticipation of one of the busiest winter social seasons in its history. New, 27-foot-long, flame-resistant nylon drapes, woven by F. Schumacher and Company, framed the 16 arched windows. The 54-foot-by-90-foot ballroom floor was completely refinished. Newly selected paint colors highlighted decorative details in the ballroom, with grayed turquoise accenting the medallions of the 20 famous women in history.

Nylon Suite. In 1948, the Hotel du Pont introduced a new deluxe suite that featured nylon furnishings throughout the rooms. Eponymously named the Nylon Suite, it featured nylon fiber in everything, including curtains, carpets, chairs, lampshades, blankets, and pillows. Even shower curtains and bath towels in the private bathroom were nylon, a novelty at the time. A "Broken Tree Stump" pattern covered the couches and chairs. The fabric earned favor in terms of durability, resistance to staining, and ease of cleaning. Nylon proved to be moth-resistant, which meant that nylon products could be stored for a long time without inspection.

Modernized Guest Rooms. Then general manager John LaMothe commissioned modernization at the Hotel du Pont. He initiated some renovations on the exterior, but he focused primarily on the guest rooms. Between 1957 and 1966, the hotel refurbished 200 guest rooms, remodeling private bathrooms and adding radios and television sets in every room.

ADDING AIR-CONDITIONING. In May 1957, management also announced the addition of air-conditioning in all 300 guest rooms and the main lobby. John LaMothe stated that the project would be complete by the spring of 1958 at a cost of approximately $500,000. The modern, all-weather ventilating system featured in newly designed hotels also helped maintain warm room temperatures in the winter.

12TH AND 13TH FLOOR ADDITION. This September 1957 photograph shows the Eleventh Street facade of the Hotel du Pont from the valet parking lot across the street. Renovations included 49 new guest rooms on the 12th floor, while the 13th floor expanded office space. This expansion completed in 1958 was the first since the 1930s.

NEW ENTRANCE. Remodeling in 1958 included a new main entrance and exterior marquee on Eleventh Street. Relocating the lobby entrance from the middle to the left of the lobby permitted guests and employees to leave the building without having to cross the lobby. A longer exterior marquee, extending 127 feet, accommodated the increased flow of cabs, town cars, and shuttles, and offered overhead protection from inclement weather.

Executive Conference Center. The Greenville Suite, shown around 1970, is just one of the many conference meeting spaces available for internal and external business meetings and social gatherings. Dark wood finishes and comfortable swivel chairs offer a relaxed yet professional environment. Located on the mezzanine level, the Executive Conference Center at the Hotel du Pont offers a self-contained, technologically up-to-date meeting area.

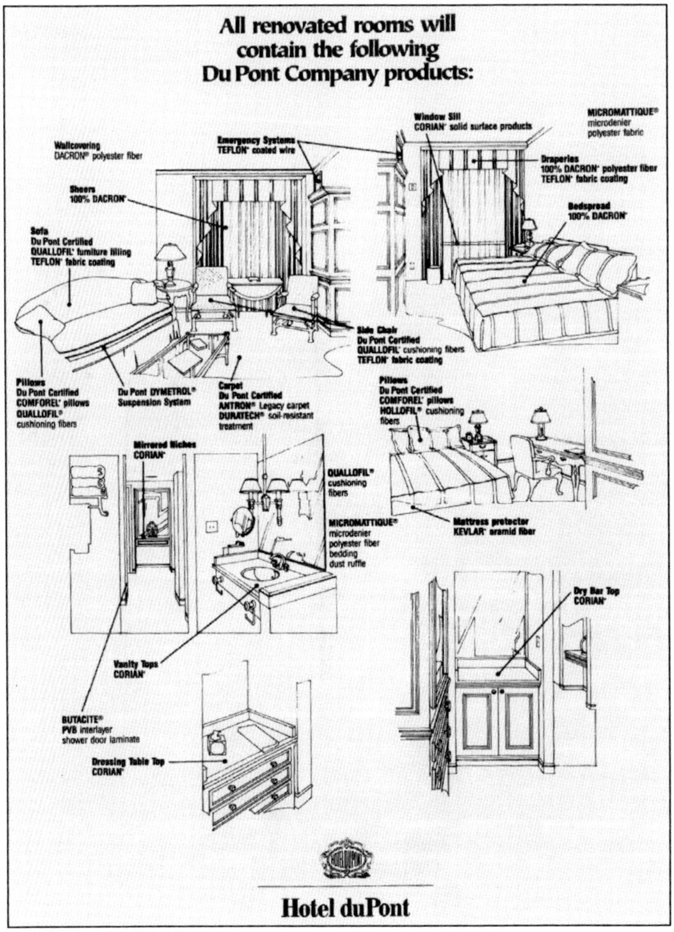

Hotel Renovations of 1992. To compete with new hotels in Wilmington, management invested $40 million in renovating the hotel in the early 1990s. Upgrades included restructuring 296 guest rooms into 217 rooms and suites and modernizing the conference center. A storyboard displayed in the DuPont Building gave visitors an opportunity to view the proposed renovations.

DuPont Materials. For decades, the Hotel du Pont has pioneered application and use of many DuPont products, from the ingredients in the kitchens and textiles in the guest rooms to paint on the walls. Products included nylon, Tontine®, Fabrilite®, Dacron®, and Duco®, for example. This sketch identified more than 20 DuPont products showcased in the 1992 guest room renovations.

Renovated Deluxe Guest Rooms. Offering a quiet retreat to work or relax, the 1992 renovated guest room, above, included built-in mahogany cabinetry, reproductions of an 18th-century, leather-inlaid desk, a separate sitting area with a glass coffee table, minibar, luxurious bathroom with separate shower and tub, queen or king bed, and mahogany nightstands with crystal lamps. However, the true favorite feature was the integrated television and videocassette recorder that swiveled 180 degrees in the entertainment unit, for viewing from any location in the room. This attractive feature and the new fine finishes earned the Hotel du Pont the prestigious Grand Prize Gold Key Award for excellence in international hotel design in 1992. The most recent renovations to guest rooms in 2006, below, updated them with new furniture, accessories, lighting, bedding, drapes, and modern, flat-screen television sets.

Conference Center. Renovated in 2012, the up-to-the-minute conference center provides current technology, modern equipment, and furnishings for businesses, employees, clients, and guests. The King Sullivan Room, shown here, features a modern drop-down screen and ergonomic chairs. Meeting rooms, reception areas, and other spaces offer light, airy paint colors and new carpeting throughout.

Hotel Lobby. The hotel lobby, as it appears in 2012, reflects interior designs that revive graceful eras of the 1920s and 1930s. Floor-to-ceiling damask drapes draw the eye to the ornately carved gold ceiling. Custom-designed floor lamps frame furniture clusters, grouped for intimate conversations. The garden-leaf carpet pattern suggests the focus of many neighboring Brandywine Valley attractions and gardens.

Hotel du Pont Exterior. This view shows the Hotel du Pont Eleventh Street exterior as it appears in 2012. Red, white, and blue patriotic banners, similar to those shown on the cover photograph from 1932, welcomed participants to a national governors' conference. The Hotel du Pont building exterior shows strength, taste, and elegance appropriate to the reputation it has earned and upheld for 100 years.

BIBLIOGRAPHY

Ayres, Harry. *Hotel du Pont Story: Wilmington, Delaware 1911–1981*. Wilmington, DE: Serendipity Press, 1981.

DuPont Building construction photographs. Accession 76.341. Hagley Museum and Library.

DuPont Central Systems and Services Department photographs. Accession 72.422. Hagley Museum and Library.

DuPont Public Affairs Department records. Accession 1410, Box 39. Hagley Museum and Library.

Fox, Marion. *Hotel du Pont and the Brandywine Valley Tradition*.Sequoia Communications Inc., 1987.

Hagley Foundation Photographs. Accession 73.201 and Accession 69.45.117. Hagley Museum and Library.

About DuPont

DuPont (NYSE: DD) has been bringing world-class science and engineering to the global marketplace in the form of innovative products, materials, and services since 1802. The company believes that by collaborating with customers, governments, NGOs, and thought leaders, we can help find solutions to such global challenges as providing enough healthy food for people everywhere, decreasing dependence on fossil fuels, and protecting life and the environment. For additional information about DuPont and its commitment to inclusive innovation, please visit www.dupont.com.